GRANNIE ANNIE'S GAP YEAR

photographs and text

by Ann Dymond

This is dedicated to Andrew, Jen, Justin and their wonderful families

CONTENTS

1 Alton

2 Basingstoke

3 Chertsey

4 Dulwich

5 Ely

6 Filey

7 Gateshead

8 Holy Island

9 Inchcolm

10 Joppa

11 Kinross

12 Laurencekirk

13 Montrose

14 Nairn

15 Orkney

16 Plockton

17 Queenzieburn

18 Rosneath

19 Sandbank

20 Tighnabruaich

21 Ullswater

22 Vaynor

23 Weston Super Mare

24 'Xeter

25 Yeoville

26 Zeal

INTRODUCTION

I was walking home one day with a bag full of fallen apples that I was going to juice, when I saw the Minden Morris dancers in the middle of Alton High Street in Hampshire. I had seen Morris dancers before, but never a women's group. For one wild moment I thought about joining them. I had just turned 80 and needed a new challenge, but not that; I couldn't dance for toffee. It looked so new, so refreshing, under my feet, in my home town. How many new things were there that I hadn't seen; wasn't it time I looked around me? I decided at that moment to have a gap year. After all, the grandchildren have them, but I missed out at that age, no one had suggested it to me, but now was a good time. I'd just go, everywhere, starting in Alton and go on to other towns around the UK using my bus pass, and my feet and maybe a train or two; I had just given up my car, so it would prove that there was life after the automobile; a strike for green freedom. But where first? As an ex teacher, the alphabet was never far away; A to Z around the UK.

I was still carrying the apples. Over the years, I have learnt how to make different brews, both alcoholic and non-alcoholic. It is not surprising that many of these drinks pertain to certain areas of the UK. I would find a drink in each town I went to. The drink would begin with the same letter as the town, to make it more interesting. Well, it would be a harmless enough occupation for someone my age and more fun than knitting and kite flying didn't really take up that amount of time

ALTON

Morris dancing has been accused of many things; bringing luck, warding off evil, engaging in fertility rites and keeping fit. Its origins are lost in the mists of time. No one even seems to know why it is called Morris dancing. The favourite theory is that it is derived from some Moorish activity in the 14th century. Be this as it may, it is now a very English living tradition and can be happened upon in many towns and villages on any summer's day.

The Minden Rose group has a further link with tradition. At the Battle of Minden in the Seven Years' War, 1756, the British and Prussian armies defeated an army of many nations. They stuck roses in their helmets before the battle and looked on them as a lucky emblem, as do the Morris dancers in Alton today. Their turquoise, shawl-collared dresses, with white aprons are modelled on the Victorian Hampshire working women's gown and they hold up garlands while they dance to the music of pipes, tabors, fiddles and button accordions, keeping wonderful time. The men's group were in variegated colours with black hats and banged sticks in a very aggressive manner. I learned that they had been on a tour to Italy, where Morris dancers do not perform every day and nearly caused a riot with their shouts and leaps. There are bells on their ankles and knees and the joy on their faces would make our doom mongers weep. The best thing is that anyone can do it; young, old, fat, thin, round, tall, short, brave and nervous. Morris dancing is an activity that stretches way back into the past, long before Shakespeare, whose Countess of Rousillon, in 'Alls' Well that Ends Well,' talks of 'a Morris for May Day'. It is an uplifting experience for those who engage in it and for those who watch on the sidelines, with tapping feet, keeping an eye open for the rain, or burgeoning of crops, whichever they please.

There is a common preconception that the only wild life worth visiting is in hot countries where the 'Big Five' survive; lion, elephant, buffalo, leopard and rhino. So, on the first day of my adventure, I take the Petersfield bus to Selborne, to walk round the Short and Long Lythes, (the rhyme with myths is appropriate) belonging to the National Trust in Selborne to follow a route beloved by the Rev. Gilbert White, who died in 1793, to prove there are other forms of wild life. While James Bruce was discovering the source of the Blue Nile and Captain Cook travelled across the Pacific, Gilbert White, who knew of these adventures stayed happily at home in Selborne, discovering, among other delights, Britain's smallest mammal, the harvest mouse. So when friends talk of overseas visits to see the 'Big Five', bring them to Selborne instead. When I stopped teaching I was given the only book White ever wrote, 'The Natural History of Selborne.' which consists of letters to two Fellows of the Royal Society, Thomas Pennant and the Hon. Daines Barrington so I know what I'm about to see, but I also pick up a leaflet at the 'Wakes Museum' in town; a memorial to the naturalist. This tells me that the little harvest mouse still shares its home with roe deer, badger, fox, squirrel, dormice and voles, which are some of the lucky creatures that live unmolested in this unspoilt meadowland. Birds were Gilbert White's first love. The smallest willow-wren, to redstarts and flycatchers are all mentioned in the leaflet as he loved the sound of their singing, particularly in summer, when the trees were too leafy to see them properly. It is not yet midsummer, so I still have a good view and although I don't find all the birds White mentions, I can hear many of them. They may not be as flashy, but they out-sing any eagle, vulture, pelican, hornbill or shrieking blue jay that may accompany the 'Big Five' in a Game Park. I begin my walk from the church, just off the main highway, finding Gilbert White's gravestone, as unpretentious as both he and the harvest mouse are. I meet two of the National Trust workers on my way round, thinning-out the undergrowth of holly, ash and sycamore, which forms an important part of an on-going programme of woodland management. This has been going on as long as people can remember and may go back as far as prehistory. It certainly was happening during the Middle Ages here in the Lythes. That is why there are still primroses jostling with wood sorrel, sweet violet, wood millet and spurge, together with all the rich flora of the meadows and ground flora of the woodland. There are plenty of trees as well, such as mature beeches that have survived great storms and diseases. Gilbert White, in his 29th letter to the Honourable Daines Barrington, in 1776, mentions that 'trees are perfect alembics:'

He noted that this ability to distil and purify water kept up the level of the Seale and Oakhanger streams, which are running happily today among the oak, hazel, beech and larch trees. The management are trying to keep or return this part of Selborne's landscape to, as near as possible, its historic state so that the species that have survived for centuries can continue to be enjoyed. An enormous number of old meadows have disappeared because of intensive modern farming methods. The National Trust acts as a guardian to protect a diversity of animal species that can compete with any 'Big Five' anywhere in the world. Well, they may not be as spectacular but it's fun looking for them. The team don't let large destructive pests get out of hand and some wish that we had the same powers in the human world. I examine fallen rotted trees that are allowed to stay where they fall, because I find ants, earwigs, crickets, worms grasshoppers and leatherjackets scurrying about. The whole area is a wonderful place for a serious naturalist and also a wonderland for younger visitors, who may safely run about on their own while exploring. You need bodyguards to visit the Big Five. There are other memorials to Gilbert White; the window in St Mary's church, Selborne, for instance, which was commissioned a century later and is known as one of the most beautiful stained glass windows in the country. There is also the Wakes Museum, administered by the Robert Washington Oates Trust, just as the National Trust looks after the Short and Long Lythes; and of course this excellent nature walk; Gilbert White's favourite. In these days of 'bigger and better' and 'more and more,' there is a reminder in Hampshire that small can be beautiful.

Back home, I'm making the local drink, apple juice. This can be done fairly easily and this way of doing it works with most soft fruit. It is not necessary to core or peel the apples. Just chop into pieces and boil in a large pan until very soft. Then put into a jelly bag or fine sieve and allow to drip into a clean bowl. Press apples slightly to encourage dripping. When all juice has been extracted, pour into bottles and keep in a refrigerator, where it should last at least a week. It also freezes well. Some people add sugar, but this depends on the sweetness of the apple and your tooth. If you have an electric juicer of course, it will save time, but they are fairly expensive and use electricity, which is not a green activity and the juice is cloudy.

BASINGSTOKE

This next town does not deserve the Edward Lear image that seems to have hung over it, especially since it became a 'New Town.'

'There was an Old Person of Basing,/Whose presence of mind was amazing/He purchased a steed/Which he rode at full speed/ And escaped from the people of Basing.'

Admittedly Lear wrote his little piece before the brilliant Anvil theatre was built.

It is not necessary today to buy a horse and ride away to escape from the people of Basingstoke. The theatre not only has excellent acoustics, staging and seating; there are shows covering music, from international orchestras to top names in jazz and pop. There are also musicals, opera, films and dance.

A friend has a quirky thought; 'it's called the Anvil, because that's where one forges a red-hot bar into a horseshoe, sword or ploughshare, a musical note cleverly used in the accompaniment to the chorus of blacksmiths in Verdi's 'Il Travatore', he informed me, without a shred of evidence. But then Neil was an opera buff and sees all from that angle. Orchestras and soloists do come from all over the word, sometimes known as Orchestras in Residence; grand title. I've heard songs from Robert Burns, Mozart and Ben Elton, a guitarist, some blues and folk music, a symphony and African singing; a good eclectic mix; lovely evenings out for everyone.   I was once privileged enough to help a group of disabled students from Treloars School in Alton give an amazing performance one night, using 'invisible instruments'; sound beams, to produce a piece called 'Twinkle', composed by the inventive musician, David Jackson. There is something for everyone.

I heard that there would be a re-enactment of an important Civil War siege in Basingstoke, which would be a good 'B'. There were to be 1,000 Roundheads and Cavaliers locking weapons in a large-scale re-enactment of an important Civil War siege in the town. They would battle on the Basingstoke Common, off Park Lane, Old Basing to mark the official re-opening of Basing House which had just had a £2.3 million facelift. They had posted a 'castle' backdrop and Basing house taster on youtube.com. and I decide to watch it. The Cavaliers have always held a fascination for me, ever since I discovered Montrose, the solder/poet who backed King Charles the First, having at first been a Covenanter. As I had been brought up by a strict Protestant father, and had subsequently strayed, Montrose had always been my hero and his town could be the 'M' on my list. Buses go to Basingstoke on the hour and I'm in plenty of time for the battle. It's enormous fun, with plenty of cannon booming, muskets firing, and sword fighting from horseback. The division between Roundheads and Cavaliers continues today, according to a Radio 4 programme in 2012 which encouraged us to take sides. We are all being persuaded to be Roundheads today, our singing and dancing days are thought to be over.

However, drinking days are never done and one of the hedgerows best offerings is blackberry cordial. There are plenty around here, so I fill a large bag and my friend who is giving me a bed for the night, and I make some that evening. We put the blackberries into a large saucepan, added one cup of water and one of sugar. (if a slow cooker is used, it is not necessary to use as much water, leave on low for about 5 hours) . Cinnamon and cloves are a tasty addition; simmered until soft then poured into a jelly bag and allowed it to drip overnight. It's not a good idea to press the fruit too hard to encourage dripping as it makes the drink cloudy. For those who prefer an alcoholic drink, brandy is a great addition which I'm sure the Cavaliers would have done.

Make blackberry jam if you like with the remaining pulp, with the amount of sugar equalling that of the blackberries.

CHERTSEY

Continuing my alphabetical way up England, I take the bus to Chertsey and the river Thames. There are more people that fish in England than play football. This astonishing fact had been made known to me earlier in the day when I arrived at the local pub. Fishing is very often free, once a rod licence has been obtained, which is not difficult or expensive. We'd been talking of Izaak Walton, who'd been a staunch Royalist and had fled to Staffordshire at the time of the Civil War because he felt London was too dangerous for him. When he had lived in London, he had regularly fished the river Lea that rises near Dunstable and enters the river Thames near Blackwell. His 'Compleat Angler' is a fishing classic as it is not just a book about fishing, but a philosophy of life, and a very green one at that. He believed that man's happiness depended on the 'happy marriage of contemplation and action' and that this was apparent in the 'most honest, ingenuous, quiet and harmless,' (except to the fish of course), 'art of angling'. There is a school of thought that believes fishing is cruel and it is possible that a hook, removed lovingly from a carp's mouth before returning the fish to water, may be construed along these lines, but the hook is small, there is no blood and fish don't scream, so most people have yet to be persuaded. The benefits of an afternoon spent by a tranquil river, costing nothing more than a hook, line, rod and some stale bread, can restore equanimity to the most restless soul. It can also offer action for twelve to sixteen year-olds, who sometimes have nothing to do after school or in the holidays.

The Environment Agency requires that everyone needs a licence to fish, as this helps them fund their work managing fisheries. It is possible to buy one at any Post Office and is advisable, as the lack would cost a fine of up to £2,500. Junior licences, bought online, cost at the moment, £5.25 for a year; under twelve's do not require a licence which is for non-migratory trout and coarse fishing. There are concessionary licences for the disabled and for those over sixty five.

Judging by the majority sitting placidly by the side of rivers and ponds, the latter are in the majority. And there is much to contemplate. The movement of the water itself, constant ripples, caused by smaller fish, such as roaches, that love to nibble the bread, a small snake can slither in from the bank, birds dive and dip to drink, mother ducks nag their babies and moorhens panic in and out.

All this is available on the Thames, now that it is so clean. In the Independent newspaper on the 30th April, 2006, it was reported that Oliver Rowe believes in sourcing local food for his new, inner-city restaurant, from the Thames, which is now 'clean and teeming with creatures.' A reporter went out with the chef and they caught 20 boxes of sprats and herrings, which is a pretty good haul, the former to fry in beer batter and the herrings to pickle or roll in oats.

The sight of a large fish taking bait, must be the second most exciting thing to happen to someone newly released from an unproductive spelling lesson, or having to read Henry V round the class. The catching of the fish is of course, the finest action of all, just look at Michael Smith's face in the picture above. There is no better advice than that with which Walton ends his book; 'be quiet and go a Angling'. With a flask of coffee beside you of course, and whether fishing, or sailing up the Thames, everyone has a thermos of coffee within reach. By the turn of the seventeenth century, there were 300 coffee houses in London. Made from a bean, discovered some say, by an Egyptian goatherd, another person who contemplates, that has become one the most favourite beans of all. Certainly, shortly after this, coffee houses began to open in London. By 1663 it is recorded that there were 82 there. The popularity of these establishments led to some opposition. For example 'The Women's Petition Against Coffee' was set up and it claimed in 1674 that coffee:-

… made men as unfruitful as the deserts whence the unhappy berry is said to be brought.

However that may be, I'm off to Dulwich, next place on the list and will go through London to check out the coffee houses available today.

DULWICH

I want Waterloo East Station in order to get to Dulwich and there are four places on the platform, offering coffee, including one with a list so long and complicated, that I find it difficult to order a plain coffee with milk.

It's hard to believe the glowing reports of the Dulwich picture gallery and I want to check out the truth of them. It is signposted all the way from the station, through the beautiful eighteenth century village of Dulwich, which was considered at one time, to have 'cleaner air' than Poland. Stanislaw Augustus Poniatowski, the last King of Poland, commissioned our art dealers, Noel Desenfans and Sir Peter Francis Bourgeois (who sounds anything but) to put together a collection that was to be a national gallery for the enjoyment of his people... Then Poland was partitioned in 1795 and there were no more kings, but Sir Peter donated his own collection of 360 paintings to the gallery with £2000 to build a mausoleum for himself and Mr and Mrs Desenfans. The present gallery was designed by Sir John Soane whose remains are also in the mausoleum.

I am happy to be one of the amazed and delighted inheritors of this wonderful establishment. There have been later additions and refurbishments, especially after a Vi flying bomb landed in Gallery road, next to the College, causing a great deal of damage. The Queen mum opened the restored gallery in 1953. Then the magical lottery came to light and Rick Mather, architect, embarked on a rebuilding project. Now there is a cafe, lecture theatre, educational facilities and the old building was given a facelift at the cost of £8.3 million. This was opened by the Queen in May 2000. Sir Peter would have been delighted. There are two paintings by Hogarth on the day I visit. One of them, 'Gin Lane' has always made me laugh, as I really enjoy a gin and I make damson gin every Christmas. I hope not to end up like the unfortunate lady on the steps in Hogarth's masterpiece. It is not too far to walk from the gallery down to Giant Arches road where I find the Sports club where they have croquet. This is a game equally hated and loved by those who have tried it and I have only recently come to terms with the fact that today it is played in a much better spirit that that which prevailed on the private lawns of choleric old gentlemen who love to hit the balls of everyone else, miles out of bounds. This is a very well known club and I was once lucky enough to have a game here with my two sons.

Back to damson gin, excellent at Christmas, or whenever the damsons are ready. Wipe the plums and take off any stalks. Prick each one with a needle; fill a jar two thirds full with fruit, than add enough sugar to come roughly a quarter of way up the jar. Use more if you have a sweet tooth and are thin enough not to worry about putting on too much weight. Mind you, the gin's full of calories, although you could bluff yourself that damsons would be one of your five a day. Fill up the jar with gin. Seal tightly and leave in a cool dark cupboard for three months. It will then be ready for Christmas. Sieve into decorative bottles if you are giving them away, otherwise put into your very own decanter.

ELY

Returning to Waterloo, I find a train to Ely, in Cambridgeshire. This is the home of Ely Cathedral, which offers an amazing sight to travellers approaching from bus or train. It is nicknamed the 'Ship of the Fens', appearing to float above the surrounding countryside. Its octagon tower is its most distinguishing feature and it also has the largest Lady Chapel in England. This is understandable, as the cathedral is built on the site of a church founded by Etheldreda the Saint. I was astounded when I read her history; a Saxon princess, born in AD630 at Exning, near Newmarket. This remarkable woman married two men, slept with neither and was made a saint. Is there a lesson here somewhere? One can understand her first husband throwing her out as she was probably too young or unwilling to share the conjugal bed, but he was a very forgiving man and gave her the island of Ely. This may have brought on her second marriage, which didn't last long as this husband released her from her marriage vows, which obviously didn't bring him the delights he hoped for either. I may have glossed over some of the details. She then founded a double monastery for monks and nuns on the site of the present Cathedral becoming its first Abbess.

The cathedral is very large indeed and needs a great deal of heating and light to make it attractive in winter time. It is better to view it at midday, even in July. Getting up too early in the morning has its disadvantages sometimes. It is not easy to find evidence of the founder, but worth the effort. A slim, white, ghostly figure, with fresh flowers at her feet is right at the end of the church, sending an aura of meekness that must cover a great strength. Christians say the meek shall inherit the earth, so perhaps she should be their saint.

Ely itself is hilly. I wander down towards the local museum to see if I can find any more information on Ely and passed Cromwell's house, which is now a tourist information office; putting him in perspective. I ask a passing lady for directions. She tells me, offering me a lift in her car and was a little miffed when I refused, explaining my reason. 'Well,' she said, 'only feet, buses and trains? It'll be a very short book.'

The gentleman running the museum is very knowledgeable; knowing all there is to know about the history of Ely from prehistoric times to the twentieth century; its tools, weapons, pottery and jewellery. the story of life in the fens and how eels are caught; a local tradition perhaps giving the town its name; Victorian laundry, land army girls, local policemen and the traumatic story of the Cambridgeshire Regiment's imprisonment in World War Two. But he had no idea where the bus stop was. 'I've never been on a bus,' he said proudly. It stopped right outside his museum.

The countryside around Ely, like most of the UK in June, is full of elderflower. They are always the basis for my favourite summer cordial. Begin by picking twenty heads of elderflower. Then bring to the boil: two pints water and two pounds castor sugar. When simmering, add one lemon and 50g citric acid (available from the chemist) . Simmer for 5 minutes, remove from the heat and add the elderflowers. Do not boil them, they do not like it. Leave for 24 hours, sieve and bottle. Store in the refrigerator.

FILEY

I make a wonderful discovery on my way to Filey. The train from Cambridge has brought me to York, and it is bit late to take a bus to the coast, where I'm heading. The Bar Convent is on the b and b list given me at the station and is just up the hill. Here I discover the oldest, active convent in the country, with padded cell and excellent breakfast. It was begun in 1686, a mere twenty eight years after the death of Cromwell, and a dangerous time for Catholics in England. There is a museum which tells the story of Mary Ward (1585-1645), the founder of a world-wide institute known as the Congregation of Jesus and the Institute of the Blessed Virgin Mary. She was a pioneer of education for women and fought for the rights of nuns to pursue a variety of ministries outside the convent walls. She was inspiration behind the present Bar Convent. These buildings are now Georgian, with an elegant Long Gallery, holding a collection of paintings related to the history of the Convent. There is a very opulent chapel, with a huge dome that is concealed from the outside world by a pitched roof, and for extra security in the event of a raid by magistrates, there are eight exits and a priest hole. There is a library of interest to students of history and religion. Of course I don't have a padded cell; I have a very comfortable standard single room, at a fairly reasonable price. The bus to Filey is as convenient as all the others have been up to date. There are 7,500 miles of coastline in the UK, they tell me, so most of us have been there at some time. My grandmother used to bring the family here from Harrogate in the early 1900's, as it has a long sandy beach, set in a wide bay, with access to some wonderful rocky pools when the tide's stopped licking at the harbour wall. There is the usual historical promenade that can be found in most seaside resorts and, best of all, there are beach huts. They are very often the reason why most of us never forget our first seaside holidays, if we are lucky enough to have a family that owns or rents one. Making sandcastles, splashing about, hunting in pools left by the receding tide, eating ices while huddled behind wind-breakers on the beach, ball games and above all, flying kites. Just standing there, holding a kite and gazing out to sea, gives a spiritual lift to me, anyway. There is also something primeval about being able to camp out, with a small primus stove and a deck chair, wriggling toes in the sand; making quick sorties to the water line; watching the abandon with which most people behave when their clothes come off; sheltered from the wind which is so good for kite-flying but dreadful to sit in. Sandcastle building is an art that occupies an entire day or until the tide comes in. It is not necessary to have a young person nearby to pretend that you are helping them. In fact it is better to do it alone; they always think they know where to put the flag, or the inner keep. They never agree where the moat should go, whether there should be a drawbridge, turrets, or which beach plants to use as soldiers, or where the water should go that leads in from a dribbling stream. Digging a tunnel right through a sandcastle is an art in itself. Judgement as to where to build the castle in the first place is the difficult one. Engineers need to keep an eye on their work of art from the hut; to watch the tide and passing beachcombers. It was gratifying to notice one grandchild, who, having ignored my efforts all day crept out while he thought I was making the tea, and shored up a portion of the moat that had fallen in.

GATESHEAD

On my way to Gateshead, I take this picture from the A1, of the Angel of the North, a sculpture designed by Antony Gormley. I stand up at the back of the bus, much to the annoyance of the driver and snap as I go past. It's a wonderful sight; made of steel and 66 feet tall, with wings measuring 177 feet across. The wings do not stand straight sideways, but are angled at 3.5 degrees forward. This, according to the notes, was done to create a 'feeling of embrace'; just the thing for a lone traveller. Why there aren't more accidents here, at the spot that marks the southern entry to Tyneside and the edge of the Great North Forest, it is difficult to understand. Because it is such an eye catcher, the Angel has served as an impetus for the regeneration of Gateshead/Newcastle, as most now refer to it. There is the Baltic Centre for Contemporary Art that is located in an old building, a riverside warehouse that remains from Gateshead's industrial past and consists of six floors of galleries, studios, study areas and a performance space. If your interest in shopping is paramount, just across the Tyne, there is the MetroCentre in Newcastle, Europe's largest shopping centre. To counteract any feeling of nausea which can accompany some people who consider shopping to be hell on earth, there are some amazing walks nearby The National Trust have a historic Gibside Estate, 300 acres of countryside, unsullied by emporiums or supermarkets of any sort. There is also Tyne Riverside Country park, which lies on the outer west edge of Newcastle, close to Newburn and the river Tyne It is easily reached by bus from town; on the day I visit, it is number 21 or 22 from the Central Station. There are miles of footpaths and bridleway that allow you to explore on foot, bike or horseback. There used to be a coalmine where the park is now and the Reigh (pronounced Reeth) is a pond that provides homes for many creatures, such as red squirrels and kingfishers. George Stephenson was married in the Newburn church and his cottage can be seen on the walk along the Waggonway to Wylam, which is two miles away. The English and the Scots had one of their regular battles here in 1640, which the Scots won and went across the ford to take Newcastle. It is now back in English hands. I had been told that if you are a bit short of cash, and who isn't? it is possible to negotiate a price with a Holiday Inn, Express. I try it and it works, but if you quote me, I'll deny it.

   I watched a programme recently where Jamie Oliver was involved with South Tyneside schools and their meals. One day a grandson, who was particularly fond of cooking, told me he'd seen my ginger beer recipe in a book by Jamie Oliver. Well, he didn't get it from me, and both he and my grandson are much better cooks that I am, but it shows I have good taste. Grate about 6 oz ginger into a large bowl. I peel it, but Jamie says you can leave the skin on if you like. It can only be grown indoors in the UK but it's available in most supermarkets. Add juice of three lemons. Pour in a large bottle of soda water. You can use sparkling mineral water, but in my day, they didn't have that. Put in about 4 tablespoons sugar; white or brown; more if you have a sweet tooth. Leave it to sit for half an hour, if your family allows you to do so, then sieve it into a large jug with ice and add a piece of mint. That's it. There are more complicated recipes using yeast, air lock bottles and things, but they are a bit fiddly.

I was going to have a Guinness because I was visiting 'G', but it only tastes really good in Ireland.

HOLY ISLAND

Newcastle to Berwick upon Tweed is less than an hour by train where two different and wonderful experiences awaited. First of all I have been told of a bed and breakfast, the Old Vicarage Guest House, at Tweedmouth, fifteen minutes walk from the bus stop and the station.

It could be the home of my Victorian grandfather, but ten times more comfortable with an en-suite room and all facilities, at a very reasonable cost. The hosts have a very welcoming attitude and breakfast was unbelievably good. There is porridge, perfectly cooked, with brown sugar, cream and a tot of whisky. That's better than a smoky cup of tea at a campsite and Ready Brek, my normal camping fare. It also sets up a traveller or pilgrim for a visit to the Holy Island, next on the list.

This is sometimes known by the original name of Lindisfarne of the famous gospels. It is said that one man probably Eadfrith, the Bishop of Lindisfarne, 698-721AD , made them in honour of St Cuthbert, another inspirational saint of the time. Northumbrian arts were famous at this time and no wonder. View the gospels at the British Library, in the John Ritblat gallery, before coming to Holy island and read that they were written on about 130 calf hides, with pens made from feathers, using black ink, which was a combination of soot and egg whites. The other colours came from plants and mineral pigments, a long way from buying a new set of propelling pencils or a handful of coloured pens at the newsagent.

It's hard for us to understand the stoicism of Eadfrith these days, but considering the isolation of the island, there probably weren't too many temptations to keep this dedicated artist from his work in the seventh century. Even today it is not all that easy to get there. I find a bi-weekly bus from the mainland which is a mere five miles across the sea. The only other way to go is on foot, but keep a good eye on the incoming tide. In 685 St Cuthbert became bishop. It was he who loved all animals and birds, particularly for some reason, the eider ducks, known as 'Cuddys'. His body, like the gospels, was snatched away from the island by monks, fleeing from the Vikings, who 'came like stinging hornets' to the church at Lindisfarne and laid all waste. Cuthbert finally ended up in Durham, where his body is to this day.

    It is a beautiful island, with a notable landmark, the lofty Lindisfarne castle, built in the 1550's to discourage Scottish raids and which became Sir Edwin Lutyens' private home in 1902. It is open four and half hours every day, depending on the tides. The island itself was founded in 635AD by St Aidan, which was the beginning of the Celtic church in England, reflected in the cross that frames St Aidan's head in his statue standing near the ruined Benedictine Priory. Pilgrims come from miles away, in their thousands, once a year, to pay homage to this holy place and all walk the original path, marked out by poles, watching very carefully, the oncoming water. As I did, when I flew my kite on the enormous expanse of clean sand, only available at low tide, on the dunes that run alongside the main access road. There are plenty of places to stay on Holy Island but I'm back to my b and b, which, after such a breakfast would surely have a good glass of wine for supper. It might even be mead.   Honey wine, or mead, is thought to have been around since Celtic days and I love the thought of St Aiden making a brew now and then. It is certainly the oldest alcoholic drink known to man and is simple to make. A combination of honey and water, fermented with a little yeast. There are more professional ways of doing this and plenty of recipes on line to follow, but I tried this at home and it was very pleasant. Some people are rude enough to say that my family will drink anything, and that may be true; but just try it. Put a gallon of water into a well sterilised carboy. Add about 4 cups of honey, (I used Manuka honey, which is expensive but worked a treat). I then added 2 teaspoons yeast, warmed up in a little water first; made a hole in the carboy lid to fit plastic tubing that leads from the mixture to an overflow jug half filled with water. Set in a cupboard, about 68 to 80 degrees, and waited for 2 to 3 weeks, checking now and then. A little fruit added is good, raisins or something that may be growing at the time. Sieve and drink; it won't do you any harm.

INCHCOLM

Inchcolm Abbey is a medieval abbey found on the island of Inchcolm in the Firth of Forth in Scotland. It takes less than an hour by train to Edinburgh which is a good centre for my next two letters of the alphabet. King Alexander 1 of Scotland (1107-24) was washed ashore on Inchcolm after a shipwreck in 1123 and took refuge in this hermit's hovel, adjacent to the present Abbey ruins.

A medieval inscription is written above the Abbey entrance:

Stet domus haec donec fluctus formica marinos ebibat, et totum testudo permabulet orbem. 'May this house stand until an ant drains the flowing sea, and a tortoise walks around the whole world'.

The Abbey is doing its best to follow the dictum as it has the most complete surviving remains of any Scottish monastic house The cloisters, chapter house, warming house and refectory are all complete and most of the remaining buildings survive. It is easy to see why St Colm chose it as a hermitage all those centuries ago and how lucky Alexander was to find shelter in his small stone building. It was the king who caused the first church to be built in the middle of the twelfth century, the nave of which stands today. There is a history of hermits who guarded this holy place, going back to the shadowy figure of St Colm. Shakespeare quotes this island in Macbeth, when Sweno, the king of Norway;

'disbursed at Saint Colme's Inch, /Ten thousand dollars to our general use...'
thus signalling the end of his battle.

There is a group of tall stones that guard the harbour and there is need for their vigilance as Inchcolm has had its share of wars, from 1296, when Edward1 of England took over, and signalled the start of battles that went on for at least three centuries. It was the beginning of the end of the monastery too, becoming a quarantine station for plague-stricken ships in the late sixteenth and early seventeenth centuries. In the 1790s a Russian hospital was set up here to serve the Russian fleet during the Napoleonic wars. In the First World War, the Firth of Forth was one of the most heavily defended estuaries in the UK, because of the naval base at Rosyth. The island was lucky to escape in the Second World War as bombs were dropped near the Forth Bridge, which was too close for comfort. These concrete and brick remains of those war time defences are an ugly contrast to the architectural splendour of the medieval Augustinian Abbey, but it is all part of the rich pattern of life. There is a rocky shore, too cramped for kite flying, but excellent for skimming stones into the sea. I manage five jumps with a real flattie. As there is only junk food available on the ferry, I save my hunger for Hawes Inn at Queensferry where Stevenson is supposed to have written 'Kidnapped' and the fish is wonderful, being so close to the sea. I try not to look across the Firth to the other side, where there is a magnificent Aquarium. It's hard to swallow fish when their relatives are looking on.

I carry water wherever I go, which was probably all that hermits allowed themselves. If I find they've been drinking anything more exotic, it will be very disappointing. It is easy to transport water nowadays as there are thousands of bottles of the stuff, sparkling or still. I do like mine cold and devised a small carrier to keep an iced bottle, which kind landladies will keep in their freezer overnight, if you ask nicely. Just sew a piece of fibreglass between two pieces of material, stitch up the sides and put a zip in the top. The frozen bottle only begins to melt when it's time for a sip. Sometimes I put a shelf bottle next to a frozen one with good results.

JOPPA

Joppa has always intrigued me, if only for its name. Myths about Scotland are fashionable at the moment, even the da Vinci code finds itself in the Rosslyn chapel, just north of Edinburgh. Comyns Beaumont's 19th century book 'Britain, the Key to World History,' does even better than that. He tells us that Jerusalem is probably Edinburgh. He 'proves' this by stating that the Palestinian Jerusalem did not conform to how the Bible describes it. Unlike Edinburgh, which does. This city, 'the 'Athens of the North,' has its Mount of Olives (Arthur's Seat), City of Zion (Edinburgh Castle) and port at Joppa. The Catrail Wall was not built by the Picts but the Romans to keep the Jews in Edinburgh. Comyns maintains that Hadrian gave orders to destroy the Jews and their city completely, leaving no trace, because they were revolting. How convenient. It was only when Constantine needed to resurrect a 'new Jerusalem' for his own political reasons he chose to locate it in Palestine. And Joppa is a very funny name, not Scottish at all, any more than da Vinci is.

The Joppa pans are only visible at low tide. Salt was mined here from about the fifteenth century until the nineteen fifties. It is difficult to find out why the sea is salt, because most of the definitions hold more information than is necessary for a lay researcher. In these cases, it is often helpful to turn to Arthur Mee's children encyclopaedias. He says it is so because all rivers run into the sea and take salt with them. That'll do for me. It probably did for Shakespeare too. His succinct 'salt of broken tears' from Troilus and Cressida, epitomises sadness in four words. Not many people can do that. Salt is made of sodium chloride, NaCl, whatever that may be. There are different kinds of salt; table, kosher, sea, and the funniest of all, that which ice cream and that which gets rid of ice on roads. It has a long history and has played an important part in the world's story. It was used to exchange for slaves in ancient Greece, hence, 'not worth his salt'. Poor old Lot's wife; she's never referred to by name, turned to say goodbye to her home and was turned into a pillar of salt

Most people, particularly those with high blood pressure, are advised against using too much salt, so I keep off it. I had just assumed that with old age, people stopped tasting food properly, until I read an article about sea salt and how chefs today believe that if you haven't seasoned food, the taste is just not there. But they use sea salt, which is what the salt pans of Joppa, near

Edinburgh used to provide. These closed when the demand fell. But according to reports, we would die without salt and people have killed for it. Ghandi used it in his long civil disobedience campaign against the British, when he led thousands of Indians to the coast to make salt from the old pans, to protest against the salt tax which had been imposed. It makes water soft and before there were more effective remedies, it preserved meat in hot climates. Biltong, strips of beef, covered in salt and hung in the sunshine, is still a delicacy for those who don't mind where the flies have been.

Joppa as an excellent sandy beach on the Firth of Forth and it is very close to Duddingstone where curling was begun in 1795, on outdoor rinks. Who will ever forget that wonderful gold medal for curling at the Olympics, even if the team never do it again? There are birds everywhere along the coast to North Berwick, where the world-renowned Sea Bird Centre has all the information worth knowing about these amazing creatures, particularly gannets and puffins, who are an example of fidelity and endurance that even the Scots find hard to equal. Here is a picture of North Berwick, taken by my granddaughter from a microlite.

It is possible to be too parsimonious on a trip like this. A friend lends me his office floor as it is Festival time in Edinburgh. The staff have gone on their summer holidays. This is a godsend, maybe not legal, but so free I can't turn it down. The offices are on the first floor of an old fashioned terraced house, south of Princes Street. I cannot believe my luck! There is a loo practically en suite and as there is no one in the building at night, I am able to use it in an emergency. There is an electronic card for entry and with one swipe, turns the red light to green for opening the door. I have my camping gear by now; so I blow up mattress, put it next to the desk, unroll my sleeping bag and I can use the electric kettle to make tea and a cup of soup. A week of bliss, with a shower at the station now and then. Then disaster strikes. I am particularly exhausted one Sunday and decide to sleep in, turning the door light red, which I haven't done before, so that no one can come in. From a deep sleep, I hear the door burst open and as I struggle to wake up, I see two men standing dramatically over my body. I don't think they have guns, but I put up my hands anyway, which looks ridiculous, as I'm in a crouched position. It takes some time to talk my way out of that. I spend the next three days at Pollock Halls, where the university is on holiday and rents out rooms to visitors. I eat my sandwiches the next day in the centre gardens of the Book Festival. while studying the programme for the day. Small children play barefoot on a large square plastic platform set in the centre. I watch a small girl sitting in the centre; 'I done a poo,' she says loudly. Her parents are occupied with bookish things so pay no attention to her. . 'I done a poo,' she says, a little more loudly. Although standing within two feet of platform, the conversation among parents continues, so there's still no attention. The child decides to investigate this poo; she finds that she has indeed done one; so she smears evidence on her leg. 'I done a poo.' She looks up expectantly, but there was still no response. In a very purposeful manner, the child totters across the plastic platform and seizes another child's rattle, finding it difficult to prise it from clenched fingers. The second child screams very loudly. All adults stop talking at once. . 'WHAT HAVE YOU DONE?' they shout. ' I done a poo,' she says, with a broad smile.

I decide to leave Joppa and its salt pans and head for my next stop, buying a bottle of juice made for sportsmen, to save myself from dehydration on the way. Sportsmen and women, including those who jog for reasons of their own, sweat more than most of us, so lose too much body fluid, including sodium and thus would suffer dehydration if they did not replace these minerals. It is possible to make your own sports drinks at home by adding a pinch of sea salt to whatever fresh juice is on the menu that day. Vegetable juice is particularly good , such as carrot, celery and spinach. A juicer is necessary for most vegetables, and may be worth the investment for your health. Bought vegetable juice is usually unbelievably expensive and will probably contain too much salt.

KINROSS

The journey to Kinross is a good example of why it is so much better to travel by bus. You can see miles further than from a car seat. The modern road bridge over the Forth of Firth that leads to Kinross opens up views, not only way down to Inchcolm Island and up past Grangemouth, but of the incredible Forth railway bridge that was begun in 1883 and finished in 1890. This used to be re-painted the moment they'd reached the end, but now they've discovered a paint that's going to last for ten years.

Kinross is a name full of history and conjures up images of poor Mary, Queen of Scots who was imprisoned in Loch Leven Castle, a remote island in the loch. There was spunkiness about Mary that makes her death a sad fact. Everybody loved her, which is probably why her cousin Elizabeth wasn't risking having her around. Mary escaped from the castle with the help of young George Douglas who was madly in love with her, but it didn't do her much good in the end. She may or may not have been fed the famous sea salmon for which the area is still famous, but it is certain that she was an early player of golf. Her attendants, French cadets, used to carry her clubs, hence 'caddies'; she played out of bunkers that had been hollowed out by sheep. Another Scottish myth? Perhaps, but there are plenty of golf courses in Kinross-shire, although I doubt if many were here at the time of Mary. These are certainly more manicured, no sheep allowed, as this is the most popular golfing centre of the world. St Andrews is to the right and Gleneagles to the left and there are at least four courses near Kinross alone. It is rumoured that golf courses ruin the environment, in that they use water that could be used for other things. I'm sure that applies to countries that suffer from drought, so perhaps golf, like whisky and bagpipes, should be confined to Scotland where there's plenty of rain. Wildlife abounds on most courses, even the links that run along the seaside, where oyster catchers find lots to eat on the greens. This certainly happens in North Berwick, where there is a wonderful three par course that used to be a women's course in my grandmother's day in the 1890's. They weren't allowed to play on the West Course with the men, but with true suffragette zeal, the women won the right to play on the main course, where the male players' worst fears were realised, as the Anderson 'ladies', one of whom was my gran, according to golf reports in the library, had the best scores on many occasions. The three par course is now for children only and you have to have one with you in order to play. If the only one available is a reluctant under 13 player who does not like golf, he or she can always read their book in the bunkers; it's one way of keeping us out of them. Just make sure they are raked smooth again. There is an honesty box here and at some other small courses in Scotland, where everyone is welcome and few don't pay.

The picture above is the head of my great uncle James Mungle, who was a much loved doctor in Kinross. He won the Practical Pathology silver medal from the School of Medicine, Edinburgh in 1883 and afterwards practised in Kinross, where they appreciated him so much they put up this drinking fountain in his honour. Any family that pass this way have to clean the bird mess off his head, which I do, much to the amusement of passersby. I have a particular fondness for this ancestor as he evidently had a friend with many blackcurrant bushes which is the basis of the drink 'Kir'. Unfortunately the friend's name is lost in the mists of time but this recipe has been passed down to us and is really easy. He was a busy man and probably instructed his wife to make it, but I have no evidence of this. Put two pounds blackcurrants into a large saucepan. Pour over 500gr sugar; 500 ml water and the juice of 2 lemons. Boil until soft, but be careful it doesn't turn into jam while you're not looking. Pour into a jelly bag and allow to drip, pressing the fruit very lightly to encourage the dripping. Leave the juice in the refrigerator until cold. It can be topped up with sparkling or still water or ginger ale. Children love it when it is poured into an ice cube tray as they enjoy sucking Kir squares. Adults put it into white wine and sometimes with good reason. They tell me it's very tasty with vodka too. I'm not sure it was called Kir in great uncle James's time, it is known in our family as 'Blackers', which wouldn't have fitted in here at all, so it's lucky it changed its name.

LAURENCEKIRK

Scottish authors understand their countryside and in 'Sunset song' the first of the 'Scots Quair' trilogy by Lewis Grassic Gibbon, whose real name is James Leslie Mitchell, this is obvious. Looking out of the coach window on the way up from Laurencekirk to explore the Howe of the Mearns, there is a shimmer of the North Sea as he notes, but in contrast to the beauty, he paints a picture of the area when it was drought-stricken;

'Up here the hills were brave with the beauty and the heat of it, but the hayfield was all a crackling dryness and in the potato park, beyond the biggings, the shaws drooped red and rusty already.'

In following the fortunes of Chris Guthrie, heroine of all three novels, Grassic Gibbon highlights the plight of many Scots; those who are torn between their love of the land and their need to find a job. Those who escape to other countries seldom lose their accents and might never return home again, but music of the pipes or a sentimental Highland lyric will reduce grown men to tears and they don't always have to have been born in Scotland. Drought was often a reason for poverty and misery in this part of the world at the time of the First World War, the General Strike and the hunger marches of the thirties. This book is a real landmark as it creates a picture of Scotland and its people at this time. To prove that Gibbon is still appreciated in the Mearns, a Grassic Gibbon Centre was opened in 1992, as a visitor centre near the Arbuthnott parish hall. It has an exhibition of the author's writing and possessions and is well worth a visit. The cafe nearby has good food too. It is however, necessary to plan very well. There is only one bus a week that will take a car-less visitor to the Centre. It runs from Stonehaven, on the east coast, where Chris, in the 'Sunset Song', visited just after her father died to make the momentous decision to keep her Blawearie farm. The name of this farm always worried me, as it seems to mean 'tired of breathing,' but I may be wrong. As a lone Scottish woman traveller, sometimes subject to 'blaweariness' myself, I identify completely with Chris. The church, with the Manse behind, still nestles in the valley below the Centre, reminding readers of the 'minister creatures' that came to try for its empty pulpit, including the one who 'wore a brave gown with a purple hood on it, like a Catholic creature and jerked and pranced round the pulpit like a snipe with the staggers'.

A memorial to this remarkable writer can be found in the corner of the kirkyard in the shape of an open book.

Wait for the only bus outside the Centre, in the road where there is no designated bus stop, and hold up one hand; two would probably be better. The infrequent arrival of the bus, underlines the remoteness of the Howe of the Mearns and the countryside 'where you'd waken with the peewits crying across the hills, deep and deep, crying in the heart of you and the smell of the earth in your face, almost you'd cry for that, the beauty of it and the sweetness of the Scottish land and skies.' (Sunset Song.) The Grassic Gibbon Centre's logo depicts the peewit, or lapwing, locally known as the peesie. Its cry is referred to in Gibbon's writing as 'an evocative image of natural permanence.' Perhaps the popularity of 'Sunset Song' is its championing of human rights and its celebration of the natural world; a good combination.

Forgive another quote from one of my favourite books, which is;

'Those folk in the byre whose lantern light is a glimmer through the sleet as they muck and bend and tend the kye, and milk the milk into tin pails, in curling froth – they are The Land in as great a measure.'

In Italy if you ask for a 'latte' you are given a glass of milk. I discovered, on being treated to a caffe latte by a grandson that a latte here, means an espresso coffee served with steamed milk. I was too polite to mention that it tasted exactly the same as the instant coffee I make at home and was twice as expensive.

I have one other 'L' drink that is so easy I make it whenever I find cheap lemons. Chop about six of them, skin, pips and all, put into a tall jug. Add a little sugar and fill up with boiling water. Leave to cool, then sieve and you have an excellent lemon drink which you need to dilute. I use the lemons about three times before I bin them. I doubt if Chris Guthrie tasted many lemons as they certainly don't grow wild in Scotland.

MONTROSE

In choosing Montrose as 'M' for the purposes of this travelogue, I have to take a trip south from Laurencekirk, which is against my rule of, 'ever onward'. I do try to go to Mar Lodge, which will mean going forward, but it is not possible, without great fortitude, to arrive there without a car. There is a post bus, which leaves about midday from Braemar, but it comes straight back and I will have to stay overnight. Most of the rooms advertised are for too many people, at least 6 to 12, self catering, and nothing suitable for a single. (I believe there are many plans in the pipeline, so check before you go, it may have improved.) I'm sorry I can't 'stride across the wild open spaces of Mar Lodge Estate, where you'll experience a unique sense of freedom.' This theme has occupied Scottish minds ever since the Declaration of Arbroath in 1320, Robert the Bruce's day, when there was trouble with the English, yet again. 'Freedom...for that alone, which no honest man gives up but with life itself.' I have devised a wonderful way of keeping up any spirits that may be flagging while striding across moors, with only deer, pine martens, red squirrels and, if you are lucky, the golden eagle to hear you; this is to sing, to the tune of Happy Wanderer.

'I like to walk along the way, to find out who is me/ And if I do it every day, soon I will be free.'

It works if you do it very loudly.

But I have spent so long in Edinburgh that I will be nearly 90 if I don't get on with it. Anyway, I need no excuse to visit Montrose, my favourite soldier/poet. James Graham, first Marquis of Montrose, (1612-1650) initially joined the Covenanters in the Wars of the Three Kingdoms, which entailed fighting between England, Ireland and Scotland between 1639 and 1651, when all three were under the rule of a single monarch and Scotland were not keen on accepting Charles 1's prayer book. The Irish Catholics rose against the English oppressors while the Civil War in England, culminating in Charles losing his head in 1649. From 1644, Montrose changed sides; maybe he was appalled at the way Charles met his death, and he fought a Scottish Civil War on behalf of the King. He has always been a romantic figure in the history books and in one of Sir Walter Scott's racier novels, the 'Legend of Montrose' set in the 1640's, full of action, death and treachery. Montrose could demand loyalty from all the chiefs of the Highlands and a more bolshie lot of soldiers could not be imagined. His inveterate and hereditary hostility to the Marquis of Argyle ensured his engaging in the war with sufficient energy and as he had enormous military talents and great bravery, he knew he could win. His statue in the square of Montrose town depicts his graceful manner, beautiful features and dignity. He wasn't all that tall, but he was well built and had great stamina, in fact he enjoyed a constitution of iron, without which he could not have endured the trials of his extraordinary campaigns, through all of which he subjected himself to the same hardships as those of the ordinary soldiers. Like all Royalists he had long hair, parted on the top of his head, which was much despised by the Puritans. Those who knew him and looked into his eyes could see that he was more than a mere soldier; he was a poet as well. ' But if no faithless action stain / Thy true and constant word,

I'll make thee famous by my pen,/ And glorious by my sword.'

These words of Montrose are cut into the plinth of his statue in the square, which proves my poetic point. Sir Walter Scott, who treats the Duke of Argyll in the 'Heart of the Midlothian' with much more sympathy, is definitely on the side of Montrose in the

'Legend'. The soldier was educated at the St Andrew's University and as Scott admired his intellect, he gave him a great epitaph in writing this book about him. Montrose's career of victories was crowned by the great battle of Kilsyth in August 1645. After that it was downhill all the way, so to speak. But it may not be too fanciful to imagine that were it not for the softening influence of poetry, Montrose could have been just as hard a general as Cromwell himself. As it was, his severed head adorned a spike in Edinburgh for many years as a warning to any other Scottish soldiers who might oppose Cromwell's merry men; and to all poets. He might not have been the first of soldier poets, but he evokes the image of war poets everywhere, such as Wilfred Owen and Siegfried Sassoon among others, who draw attention to the futility and horror of war.

It was ironical that Montrose was executed in the same way as the king for whom he'd fought so hard. He wrote this poem the night before he had his head cut off in Edinburgh, in 1650, having been betrayed by McLeod of Assynt, who surrendered Montrose for a large sum of money. The McLeod name still stinks in some parts of Scotland.

'Let them bestow on every airth a limb,

Then open all my veins, that I may swim

To thee, my Maker, in that crimson lake,

Then place my par boiled head upon a stake;

Scatter my ashes, strow them in the air.

Lord, since thou knowest where all these atoms are,

I'm hopeful thou'lt recover once my dust,

And confident thou'lt raise me with the just.'

I found a record of my great grandfather, rector of St Baldred's Episcopal Church in North Berwick, Scotland, having put his name down on a subscription list in the 1870's, for the poems of Montrose and I can understand why.

I have a very comfortable night at the Best Western Hotel, which is good value here and also in the States, where I stayed at the Los Angeles airport BW hotel while visiting my great aunt, Diana Anderson, the daughter of the Scottish rector. Diana and the Duke have one thing in common, they never give up, like a mule, which is why I ordered her favourite drink from the bar; a Moscow Mule .   When Diana was 85, she came with us for a visit to a game reserve in Africa. She caused a minor sensation in the primitive bar the first evening, when she ordered a Moscow Mule. As no one had the faintest idea what she was talking about, she proceeded to explain. 'Ginger beer and lime juice,' she said. When this was produced without too much difficulty, after all, limes grow in abundance in Africa, she added; 'Of course, some people add vodka.' The colonial bar brightened up and it was Moscow Mules all round.

NAIRN

From Aberdeen bus station Stagecoach will take the pretty way to Nairn, a seaside town on the Moray Firth. This is a three hour journey, full of wonderful views through Keith and Elgin and the Speymouth Forest, to the Cairngorms covered in snow. Or you can take the train which takes two hours to Inverness and then on to Nairn. This is also Macbeth country and little Erica can be seen admiring Cawdor Castle, only four miles away from Nairn.

From the train, there are views of fallen sheep -folds, scattered around like children's bricks forgotten at night, through wonderful names, Pitlochry, Dunkeld, Blair Athol, Dalwhinnie, Newtonmore, Kingussie, all of which have Gaelic names printed alongside, such as the last, which is Ceanna Ghiuthsaich; difficult for the English tongue to pronounce.

I have a bagful of seedless grapes with me, one of my five a day, but when they push past with the coffee tray, carbohydrates all the way, under the icy Highland skies, one really needs some greasy chips. I apologise to myself. A valley of ferns glides past and the purple loosestrife! It covers everything, garish in the pale green grass, waving their heads this way then that. Rain slants on the train windows, making them looked cracked, as if someone is hurling stones. Sheep stand dead-still, with noses pointing to the storm. There are some bright, blue quad bikes, a modern anachronism, roaring round a square field under screaming jets.

But suddenly Nairn is there; known sometimes as Brighton of the north. I stand hopefully on the sandy beach, waiting for a dolphin to rear its beautiful body, but no luck. It is a normal sight here, as the Moray Firth is home to one of only two colonies of dolphins in the UK. I am told others often see them. Nairn has also an active harbour, with many sailing clubs and some offer trips to sea for those who might enjoy it. It is easy to find the seashore. Just stroll down Harbour Street, the name should give a clue and enjoy the small shops all the way, proper seaside ones, which sell buckets, spades and kites, there's a post office, a tattooist, caffs, ice cream and even a bridal shop. The beach is often chosen as a suitable wedding venue and dancing barefoot on the sand, after the ceremony, not during it, has cemented more than one permanent alliance. This one was taken on a warmer beach but they are all wonderful

Cawdor Castle has a magical name linked with Macbeth by Shakespeare and is only four miles away. It was built in the 14th century as a private fortress by the Thanes of Cawdor. Nairn has overcome its close association with tribal warfare even though Cullodon Moor, where the last land battle took place on mainland Britain is not far away. Here the Jacobites took their final beating in 1745, falling in a battle for what they believed in, as Montrose had done a hundred years before. Bonnie Prince Charlie didn't manage to bring the Stuarts back to the British throne, even though he was just as romantic a figure as Montrose had been. He would have approved of modern Nairn, with its wide range of popular activities such as folk nights, ceilidhs (kalies) and jazz music, the book and art festival in May, theatre and even cookery evenings, maybe featuring that wonderful Scottish chef, Nick Nairn, who, now I think about it, looks a little like Montrose. There's Highland Games as well, a much more civilised, on the surface anyway, battle of physical ability, especially the caber tossing, which reveals more Highland muscle than thought possible. There is plenty of public transport available in Nairn, which makes it a popular place for single, spur-of-the moment travellers. Find the bus that goes to Grantown-on-Spey, south of Nairn, which is the beginning, or the end, of the whisky trail leading to Cromdale, Ballindalloh,

Aberlour, Craigellachie, Fochabers, Elgin, Forres and back to Nairn It is not necessary to visit each distillery, if you don't want to, just spend the day in Grantown and sample some of the delights of the world's most famous drink. Taken in moderation, I believe, it is good for most things and try as they might, the rest of the world cannot produce a compatible copy, although the Irish might say they invented whisky, no one believes them; it doesn't even taste like the real thing and they spell it with an 'e'. The Queen also gets in on the act. The Glenlivet and Fochabers Estates total 71,000 acres of Sovereign property whatever that may mean. For a period, the Speymouth Forest was part of the extensive lands of the Dukes of Gordon . They were short of a bob or two and sold the standing timber to a shipbuilder in 1785. I wish I could have seen the 'floaters' sliding logs into the Spey, sometimes 20,000 at a time, especially as part of their payment was free whisky.

Some of the enmity between England and Scotland today is over whisky, among other things. It is said that the whisky reserves in warehouses are worth more than the total gold reserves of Great Britain, which is not difficult to believe at the present time. The famous Glenlivet was one of the first illegal 'stills' to become legal and still epitomises the best of the 'aquavitae' known to the world.

There are those that can walk and fish this trail, but it is too long for me. I take the bus to Spey Bay, with the mountains behind me and thought I may be lucky enough to see ospreys hovering over the river choosing their salmon dinner, but I'm not. The North Sea is ahead and the far coast of Caithness. If only the dolphins would go past now, but the sunset almost makes up for it.

I'd done a little whisky tasting during the day and didn't feel like any more that evening and decided to have some nectar instead. According to mythology, this was the drink of the gods. It may not sound much, but after a long day on the golf course, walking along the beach, or exploring Nairn, it tastes divine. Fill a glass half full with lemonade, half soda, put in a drop or two of angostura bitters and top with a slice of lemon. Add ice if you like. This is known as a rock shandy, but I call it nectar.

ORKNEY

There are buses and trains to Inverness the next morning, in plenty of time to catch the train to Thurso, where the ferry leaves for Orkney. This journey is up a ladder of really evocative names. Beauly (A'Mhanachainn) , Muir of Ord, Dingwall, Alness, Invergordon (two oil rigs in the distance), Fearn,Tain, (golf courses glimpsed), Ardgay. Once again we are sailing along on a sea of cerise purpleloostrife. Culrain (part of the national cycle network), Invershin, Luirg, Rogart, Golspie, Dunrobin Castle (falconry), Brora, Helmsdale, Kildonan and Kinbrace, Forsinard, Georgemas Junction, a bleak place where they change drivers and on to Thurso or John 'o Groats. I take the former for Stromness and the ferry.

It is well to warn travellers of all kinds, young, old, rich, indigent or just plain foolhardy, that it is not worth while crossing the Pentland Firth to Orkney unless they either have a car, or intend to hire one. It is the worst possible place to test any other kind of transport. The only alternative is to organise a coach tour with soul mates. Individual, on-the-spur travel is not recommended.

The second warning also comes from personal experience. Do not attempt to camp unless using a state of the art caravan or camper home. Tents find it difficult to stay up in the driving rain and wind, which might quite possibly be prevalent at the time. On this particular visit, it was more than present, it is overpowering. As soon as the tent is up, and it's not a big one, the wind hurls it down again, as if it had some particular spite against me. Even with the help of some very accommodating Germans, who are experts at this sort of thing, it is impossible. They shake their heads in disapproval and swear in the most colourful way. I have to give up and find a b and b. However, if you have a car and it's not raining, it is camping heaven.

There are quotations from George Mackay Brown, the famous Orkadian poet, engraved on the glass partitions of the Hamnavoe ferry that crosses over to Orkney.

'the essence of Orkney's magic is silence, loneliness and the deep marvellous rhythms of sea and land, darkness and light.

I can go along with all that. One of the joys of travelling alone is that no one can distract from the shape of a cloud or the childish scribble, drawn on a darkening sky that they say is the Old Man of Hoy. Shrill blasts of mobile phones on the lurching deck, with seagulls beating their wings furiously against waves that rise dangerously high, can be tolerated if the agony is not compounded by two people having to endure them. It is also very important indeed, when dragging a wheeled case containing tent, blow-up mattress and sleeping bag; backpack becoming heavier by the minute, along stone squares, in clanking, drizzling misery to the campsite, which is 'only a pace or two along the High Street' a lie if there ever was one, it is doubly important as I say, to be alone. All rage, fury, impotence and language that have lain hidden in primeval depths come to the surface and it is not a pretty sound. Back to bed and breakfast at the Ferry Inn then.

There is disappointment that accommodation plans have fallen through but exploration is still to come. Tomorrow Kirkwall and the Italian chapel, which takes a very pretty picture, built by prisoners of war; and all the birds that are rumoured to be about, including puffins. There's Skara Brae, the Stone Age village which can blow your mind, the ring of Brodgar, the Neolithic village with the Standing Stones of Stenness from the third millenium BC and Scapa Flow, which brings back tearful wartime memories. The bus leaves for Kirkwall on time, right outside the Inn. Perfect. Grey sweeps of water in the sky and on the ground fill large flat lochs and the Stromness Golf Club looks more like a lido. Little grey smallholdings dot the landscape and miracle! the sun comes out briefly to reveal a glimpse of Rousay and Egilsay islands before the bus falls back into the clouds again on the way to Kirkwall. Here, there's the grand St Magnus Cathedral and a crumbly Earl's palace, but before exploring either, I want to have a look at the Italian Chapel, which is out of town. However, there is only bus going that way in an hour's time, which will give a ten minute stop at the chapel before going on to the ferry at Burwick, which sails to John o' Groats. Three hours later, the bus will return.

Luckily there's a magnificent library in Kirkwall and after a thorough inspection of the cathedral and palace, both of which very rewarding if you have the time, I catch up on email and check the bus times again. Much more organisation is needed before coming again, which I certainly will.

The island will repay with sights of a rich and varied wildlife, birds and archaeology to die for. Many people did. But there's only time for me to take the bus back to Stromness and the Ferry Inn, where, after an excellent hot shower, over my wonderful supper of scallops and new potatoes, I sit near a table of eleven, very jolly people.

'What is it about Orkney that makes you enjoy it even in this driving rain?' I ask.

'We're divers,' they said.

I'm given a most delicious oatmeal drink before I go to bed. I ask for the recipe and here it is; Soak one cup of old fashioned rolled oats, with a cinnamon stick, in 4 cups of water for 30 minutes. Then blend all (the cinnamon is optional), strain and sweeten with sugar or honey. I swear there was a tot of whisky in it as well as I sleep very well

PLOCKTON

I catch the ferry back to Thurso on my way to find 'P'. It's time to go down the west coast of Scotland now, and there, just in the right place, is Plockton, on the opposite coast to Skye. One of the more enjoyable series I watched on TV was Robert Carlyle in 'Hamish Macbeth' . No relation to the famous King. Scottish City Link buses run most of the way to Plockton, leaving at 9 o'clock in the morning and arriving at Inverness at 12.33, which gets me the connection to Invergarry and then to the Kyle of Lochalsh. From here to Plockton it is a mere 15 minutes by train. There is also a magnificent Inverness to Kyle of Lochalsh scenic railway that can be enjoyed instead of the coach trip. This passes castles, rolling landscapes and wild mountain scenery, such as the Achnashellach Forest which is full of spruce, willow, oak and holly and Attadale, where the Vikings fought ferocious duels and held sporting events. You can see Plockton as you approach the Kyle of Lochalsh, in the shelter of low hills. Even car-lovers will take hours to reach the hamlet from Glasgow and it is two hours from the nearest airport. The buses let you enjoy the scenery of the Scottish Highlands all the way there, as does the train, which shortens the journey considerably.

If you want to have a taste of Plockton before visiting it, watch the video of 'Hamish Macbeth' which is still available. But it's worth travelling the extra mile to see such spectacular scenery for real. The village hall is there, as is the shop, the sailing club, pub and about 100 local volunteers who were extras, all of which made a good profit, making up for the disruption. If crime is not your scene, don't let it worry you, keep your eye on the background and Robert Carlyle is worth sixty minutes of anyone's time, whatever age they may be and whatever he may be doing.

In reality it is better to visit the attractive stone-built Plockton Hotel which stands only metres from Loch Carron, warmed by the Gulf Stream and fringed with palm trees. Sit, looking across the bay to the castle and the Applecross Hills, while eating either whisky pate, freshly landed Plockton prawns, trout, scallops, herring in oatmeal or Highland venison casserole with red wine, juniper berries and redcurrant jelly; leave room for the pecan, whisky and maple tart. There is, of course, a fine range of Highland malts to choose from. Prawns are landed daily at the harbour and other seafood comes from Mallaig or further north from Kinlochbervie, where scallops are hand-dived. Mussels come from Skye, visible across the Inner Sound. No one does food better than the Scots and I'm not biased.

This small lochside hamlet is an idyllic place and could be the template for all chocolate box pictures. There is a row of neatly painted cottages along the shoreline of the tiny harbour. There are palm trees along the main street, and they are framed by heather and pine in a craggy landscape behind. It is heaven for artists now, but was used as an embarkation centre for those who were thrown out during the infamous Highland Clearances in the 18th century and who went on to make a new life in the new world. Its original name was Am Ploc, which is far more fun than Plockton.

It's worth doing a second 'P' here and taking a bus across to Portree, the capital of Skye. Now that the bridge has been built, City Link buses chortle along happily, leaving frequently and taking only about an hour to reach Portree Square. There are excellent b and bs to be had in the town and in the summer months, wonderful walks and views of the grand Cuillin hills around . There were plenty of attractions in town; Scottish dancing, an accordion and fiddle competition, a garden fair, pipes festival, a marathon, archery and Highland Games. There is also the Plockton regatta, which takes place over two weeks on the seafront, very popular with seafarers from all over the world. Gaelic suddenly becomes relevant. There is nothing more important to the Gaels than belonging to something, somebody or somewhere. 'Ca leis a tha thu?' roughly translated means, 'Who do you belong to?' According to these warm and lovely people, we all belong to someone, which is comforting, even if sometimes this is difficult to prove. For instance, Domhnall Mhurchaidh Dhomhnaill Ruaidh is: Donald, son of Murdo, son of red-haired Donald. It may have been more than a hundred years since Donald had red hair, but that is who he belongs to. Children are very important to Gaelic people and the clan system was the basis of family life. Today they are still very important in the scheme of things, as the emphasis on education proves. Parties are also popular, ceilidhean , they call them, which is a real Scottish social gathering with lots of music and dancing. Here there is very often a party punch served. I doubt if it follows one that was popular in Jane Austen's day, called negus.

To every pint of port allow one quart of boiling wine and water in equal parts and put into a large jug. Rub the sugar well into the rind of the lemon until it becomes yellow, than add it to the water and wine, straining the juice from the lemon as well and grate in some nutmeg. When it has cooled a little, the drink is ready. This was often drunk at children's parties, so they used a fruity wine, like port. And they accuse our teenagers of drinking?

QUEENZIEBURN

Once back at the Kyle of Lochalsh, the train goes to Glasgow, where I shall stay at the university rooms that are available during the holidays. I've worked out a very pleasant Q,R,S and T, which are all close by and as I have a cousin who lives in T, it will be a good chance to visit. Queenzieburn is the first on my list, reachable by bus from Buchanan bus station in Glasgow, (do not pronounce the 'z'; they don't in Scotland, as in Menzies). It is a friendly village between Kilsyth and Kirkintilloch in a stunning natural setting under the Kilsyth hills, where it is possible to look up and imagine Montrose swashbuckling his way against the Duke of Argyll. There is not much in Queenzieburn other than a pub and the village school, but its most important feature is the fact that it is the starting point for fine walks in all directions. Most people from the surrounding towns and villages make camping and walking a weekend excursion and if I had my tent with me, I would love to do that and perhaps find a jasper cave among the rocks. My favourite piece of jewellery is a small pendant, given me by my daughter Jen, made from this semi-precious gemstone that is much prized in the lapidary trade. I walk up the Tak-me-Doon road, (mind-boggling where that name came from?) past the golf club and follow the path by the burn. I don't have time to take the Tomtain, which is 453 metres high, the most easterly of the tops and will give great views to the east and I don't find any jasper either. It is not certain when it was first worked here, but the nearby valleys of the rivers Blane and Kelvin are rich in Celtic and earlier sites. Just to the south ran the Roman Antonine Wall. In the late 18th century, the German mineralogist Rudolf Erich Raspe was reported to have found red and yellow jasper near Kilsyth. Since then jasper has been collected in the Campsies and I might have found some if I had been able to walk further and higher into the hills, keeping my head well down.

Here it was too, that Montrose defeated the Covenanters, under Baillie, who were actually occupying the more advantageous position on the east hills of Kilsyth. Montrose was camped with his army in low-lying fields in the basin below, in other words, Queenzieburn. (I made that up, as it isn't mentioned anywhere, but it is possible.) The covenanters were split in their plan to defeat Montrose. Some came down to the valley, while others waited for reinforcements above. The soldier, rather than the poet, took advantage of this and attacked, sending Baillie's troops flying back to Berwick, while Montrose marched triumphantly into Glasgow, claiming it for

Charles 1st. It is easy to walk down the single road through Queenzieburn and hear the victorious Highland pipes, which is where they sound encouraging, as in battle, which I haven't experienced, and outside, which I have often, with pleasure and pride.

I buy a bottle of quince juice on my way back to the university. Fruit grows more slowly in Scotland and has a better flavour than any grown down south. Quinces are a good example of this and I often make quince juice which is delicious with Bacardi or on its own.

Skin, core and chop 2 medium quinces; put them in a saucepan with 3 ½ cups cold water, 1 cup fresh lemon juice and 2 ½ cups sugar.

Simmer until soft then strain through a jelly bag, pressing pulp slightly to encourage dripping. Serve cold with ice and a slice of lemon. I drink my bottle warm tonight out of my tooth mug and it's still pretty good.

ROSNEATH

Unfortunately the day I go to Rosneath, the weather does not live up to the reputation that Sir Walter Scott gives it in 'The Heart of the Midlothian.'

'In these isles, the severe frost winds, which tyrannise over the vegetable creation during a Scottish spring, are comparatively little felt.........and the air is also said to possess that mildness which is favourable to consumptive cases.'(Ch. XL11, Heart of the Midlothian, Sir Walter Scott)

I am wearing every bit of warm clothing that I possess and feel that the symptoms of consumption, whatever that may be, are imminent. The train from Glasgow takes me to Gourock and to Kilcreggen, which leads on to Rosneath, or Roseneath; the former is the more usual Scots way of pronouncing it, although Sir Walter used the latter in his book, when he sends Jeanie Deans there under the protection of the Duke of Argyll, who is, nearly two centuries later, a more kindly soul than the one who incurred the wrath of Montrose in 1645.

It is hard to see the ferry at Gourock, as it's so small there is very little showing above the harbour wall and because the sea was extremely rough on this particular day, I feel rather like Scott's Mrs Dutton, who was to be in charge of the 'cow-milkers' on Inverary and who was appalled at the '**wild men with their naked knees and of this nut-shell of a thing, that seems bobbing up and down like a skimming-dish in a milk-pail.**' There are no naked knees on the day I take the ferry, I can tell you. Scott sets this part of the story in Rosneath, in 'picturesque beauty' of an island, which is not far from the Holy Loch. There are still weeping-willows and birches, as the air is normally mild, with plenty of gorse about. From Kilcreggan it is a picturesque walk to Rosneath along the banks of the Clyde, less than three miles away. It is only one and a half miles by the main road, but as one friendly coal merchant tells me, that it's far too dangerous to walk. 'Cars' he said, 'are not to be trusted.' A man on the green side; but I'm not sure how he delivers his coal.

From the site of the old Rosneath pier, where I can almost see Jeanie Deans in her 'shock of surprise' at being carried ashore by the rowers, it is possible to look back at the winding path that follows the line of the Clyde. Just above the pier is the old Ferry Inn, which, in my ignorance I had hoped would be a cheery pub, with some good food. But it hadn't been a pub since anyone could remember. It was originally one of only two houses designed by Edwin Lutyens in Scotland. It was built for Princess Louise (daughter of Queen Victoria) on her marriage to the Marquis of Lorne. This is great camping country too, as Rosneath Castle, a seat of the Duke of Argyll, was burnt down in 1802 and is now a neat and tidy park with plenty of room to pitch a tent, it has a good shower block, and is a perfect place to be should the 'haar' come down and you can't see your hand in front of your face. There's a good on-site shop and laundrette with a pub and restaurant. The views are stunning and flying kites is a must. Camping is much easier these days, and I can fit a small blow up mattress, plus its battery powered pump, a sleeping bag and folding tent into a pull-along case. I do not have it today.

St Modan's churchyard in Rosneath, is full of dead Campbells, closely related to the Argylls, with an Anderson or two and one Robert Story, a slave from the trade that we're all ashamed of now. But he was given a great tombstone which nestles below the glens, lakes and waterfalls where Lady Staunton (Jeanie Deans sister) goes for walks with her nephews and is rescued by her long-lost son. It is a country of Romance and on this magic peninsular, anything is possible.

It is the time of rosehips and there are plenty on the bushes on my walk back to Kilcreggan. Rosehip syrup was given to me as a child and I gave it to my children as it is full of vitamin C. This is how to make it, which is much cheaper and tastes far better. Pick a kilo of rosehips; put into a pan of 2 litres boiling water. When it has boiled, leave to stand for about 15 minutes then pour the pulp into a jelly bag and strain. Boil the pulp again in 1 litre water this time and strain as before. Do this three times and the third time put into half a litre water and add 500g sugar. Bring to the boil and allow to stand for 15 minutes then strain. Bottle all the resulting liquid when cool and put in the fridge. Brilliant; don't add any alcohol, it ruins it.

Before I visit 'S', I will spend another night in Glasgow for a very special reason. Museums very often share space with art galleries, or libraries and will live for ever, especially ones like Kelvin Grove. I have arranged to meet my grandson who is filming in Glasgow, with his wife, Jo, son Finn and daughter Mimi, who love the Spitfire hanging above a field of wild animals, all eyeing each other with a view to their own survival. Everyone can find something to enjoy here, from four to eighty four and probably more, but I can't speak for them although I see many of all ages, with big smiles on their faces. Mimi tries on as many high heeled shoes as she wants and totters about, trying to copy mother. Finn sits down to draw a tree under the eye of a natural-world expert, while Mimi makes a montage composed mostly of pink tulle. It pleases her enormously.

SANDBANK.

To reach Sandbank, my 'S', it is a necessary pleasure to spend another night in the Glasgow university room and then catch the ferry from Gourock to Dunoon. It is an easy walk to Sandbank along the banks of the Holy Loch, to catch a bus, one of which had this sign over the driver's head that announced; 'All unaccompanied children will be sold as slaves'. The Holy Loch Marina has all the sailing and yachting facilities you would expect to find in a first class marina. The scenery is magnificent, as it is the gateway to the Highlands on the Cowal peninsula where the land meets the sea. It is also a very secure haven for sailing. This is another very popular British pastime; surrounded by the amount of sea we have, this is not surprising and there are very few places on the coast that don't have a marina of some sort or another. I read today that a town in England, 100 miles from the sea, has formed its own yacht club. But they may have more money than sense. This cliché was one of my gran's favourite sayings, another was 'you never know your luck 'til you tread in it' and when on a journey such as mine, this has never seemed more true.

Sailing has always looked very romantic to me, but it always looks an expensive pastime. However, as many sailors spend a whole day just scraping, painting and mending sails, there is pleasure in most things, even if you have to tread in it before you find it.

I have left Dunoon and the statue of Highland Mary that stands on the cliff overlooking the town and who, according to the locals, was the love of Robert Burns's life. There is doubt about this in some quarters, as Jean Armour, his wife, put up with quite a bit from the poet, but remained faithful to him, which is more than he did to her. It may have been guilt that inspired Burns to write 'Highland Mary' when he was fairly young and certainly as irresponsible as he ever was. Mary, who according to legend, was 'tall, fair haired with blue eyes,' was bound to attract the poet. She died of a fever while waiting for Burns to meet her at Greenock, where it is said, they were going to elope to Jamaica. It is difficult to imagine Rabbie Burns out of Scotland and it is probably better to draw a veil over this particular hiccup in his eventful life. It was during a period when he was battling on the family farm, south of here, in Ayrshire. There is sometimes sadness in his poetry, underlying the magic of it and this may be because of Mary. They did find a small infant coffin in her grave when it was opened up, which could have been the reason for her death.

Our parting was fu' tender;/But Oh! Death's untimely frost/That nipt my flower sae early! Now green's the earth and cauld the clay/That wraps my Highland Mary!'

We quote Burns on many occasions, once a year anyway, when 'Auld Lang Syne' is bellowed out on December 31st. He was a passionate believer in the equality of men, though I'm not so sure of his views in this direction in the case of women. He was a very attractive man and led a fairly dissipated life, when he wasn't collecting and writing Scottish songs, including the one that celebrated the passing of a year and 'O my love's like a red, red rose.' 'Ye banks and braes' and 'Scots wha hae' all of which, like bagpipes, can reduce grown men to tears, particularly on Burns night, January 25th, his birthday and not only Scotsmen weep. Burns' Night supper usually adopts this menu; 'cock o' leekie, tatties and mash, roastit beef, haggis, dunlop cheese and whisky'; a tasty lot.   There aren't many poets that have a day named after them and which is kept with such enthusiasm and I doubt if there are many students in Britain who haven't had 'the best laid plans of MICE AND MEN , gang aft agley' explained to them as they battle through this Steinbeck novel , prefaced with the truthful quotation.   The passengers on my bus are a very knowledgeable lot on the day I catch it to go to Tighnabruaich, winding over the hills on the Cowal Peninsular. They quote Burns and Shakespeare, outdoing each other in stories of the old days, while the friendly driver stops to pick up people on the roadside, whether there was a bus stop there or not. As it was the only bus of the day, that was lucky. Small buses are very friendly, which is another good reason to use them to get from A to B, let alone A to Z . They are economical on the pocket too which is why I often take the overnight coach if I have a long trip to do; it's full of students and people in a hurry. A grandson, who is no respecter of persons, once told an assembled party that his grandmother always took the bus because she could have a bottle of sherry with a straw on her lap. Scurrilous slur, but not a bad idea now I come to think of it. Sherry is a good drink for pouring into soups too and another good idea for Christmas ; Fill a bottle half full with hot chillies; use red ones because they look good when topped up with pale dry sherry, particularly if you are using a clear glass decanter. The longer you are able to keep this, the hotter it becomes and a drop or two is good, not only in soup, but in stews as well. Not bad in spag bol either.

TIGHNABRUAICH

I am lucky to have a few days with Mary my cousin, who says I may stay as long as I please. But my father used to say that guests and fish stink after two days, a good rule to follow. This area is sailing heaven and has seen hundreds of different types of craft that have wandered in, from ancient and medieval sailors to modern yachts. There is an excellent society in Tighnabruaich that is dedicated to preserving the pier so that one of these boats in particular, the 'Waverley' which was the first post war passenger boat built on the river, can come in to pick up passengers. . She is now the last traditional Clyde steamer in operation. They are not considered an economical form of transport today, but the Waverley has earned her keep by travelling from the Clyde to the south of England, the Bristol Channel to East Anglia and even to the north of France. She has sailed right round Britain several times. the Pier Association of which Alan was an active member, (see 'Kyles and the Sea' by Alan Millar) keeps the original wooden pier in good nick and reminds local politicians occasionally that it is in their interest to keep the pier sound enough to attract the thousands of visitors that use the Waverley to call on Tuesdays and Saturdays from late June until the end of August.

The steep road from Sandbank to Tighnabruaich is not too busy, which is lucky, as it is single lane in parts It also means that many people miss out on seeing the most spectacular and rugged scenery in Scotland or for that matter, anywhere. The Gulf Stream current ensures a mild climate here, as in Plockton and it is a perfect setting for walking in the heather-filled moors above the town. Golf is popular here too, as it is all over Scotland. There is an excellent course just above Tighnabruaich, with views over the Kyle that make it difficult to keep one's head still.

And as for kite flying! It has to be said that the wind can be gusty here, but a walk to Ardlamont Point, where the Kyles meet Loch Fyne, should be where an international kite flying competition takes place; perhaps something on the lines of the one that the Afghan kite-runners take part in? The warm waters on the Firth of Clyde are excellent for sea angling. There are many rocky outcrops along the coastline that are easily accessed and give plenty of opportunity for catching mackerel or conger eels. In the forested hills of the Cowal peninsular there is angling for salmon, trout and powan, a freshwater white fish, while Loch Fad on the Isle of Bute, again amongst superb scenery, is famed for its rainbow and brown trout. Lochs Ascog, Qien and Greenan, again on Bute, are excellent for coarse fishing and fine specimen pike are a rich prize at Ascog.

There are, I am told, 750 Scottish islands. Not all are inhabited but one not far from here is Islay, the southernmost island of the Inner Southern Hebrides and lies in Argyll and Bute. It is pronounced Eye-la and the first reference to it comes in a biography of the Irish saint Columba, in about 729AD when he visited the Islay on his way north, prior to founding the famous monastery on the Isle of Iona, off the south-west tip of the Isle of Mull. I visited Islay years ago on a tiny plane, that had a propeller, which flew from Glasgow. I was to take pictures of the island from the air, but it was so overcast on the day we landed and the day we took off, that the only shot I got was through the propellers in the one moment the sun came out. The island is largely composed of peat and the water is brown, even the water in the burns. There are eight distilleries on the island; all coastal and battered by the sea winds which drive salt spray far inland which saturates the peat. This is dried again by the briny, seaweedy breeze. All these characteristics go into the whiskies of Islay which are the strongest flavoured of all malt whiskies, which are either loved or loathed.

Mary is a great gardener and can grow almost anything. Her greenhouse is full of tomatoes at the moment, so I make myself a wonderful cocktail. We just cook tomatoes, skinned but not seeded, plus a celery stick and an onion, until soft in a little water. Once liquidised, I strain it all, adding a little salt, pepper and Worcestershire sauce, into a long glass. It can be diluted with water, when it is a tomato cocktail, or with vodka, when it is a Bloody Mary, not, I assure you, named after my cousin.

ULLSWATER

Back then to Glasgow, where I plan to spend two nights at one of the University residences so that I can visit the wonderful Kelvin Grove again and the Mitchell reference library. Then I take the train from here to travel to the Lake District and 'U', to have a look at more steamers and more spectacular scenery. Penrith is on rail from Glasgow and a bus takes me to Pooley Bridge Steamer Pier on the edge of Ullswater. The bus only takes twenty minutes to the lake and has to hoot at sheep most of the way down. The steamers are now diesel, which is a disappointment; the only steam ferry left, the 'Gondola' is on Coniston water. but 'Lady of the Lake' which called for us was 35 years old when the Titanic was sunk and gives us a graceful sail round the seven and a half miles of Ullswater.

Helvelly mountain is visible from Pooley Bridge and for those who can manage a 3250 climb, it may be attacked from Glenridding, where we are heading on this ferry. Sitting comfortably on a ferry is an excellent way to see the Lake District, with sudden small glimpses of horses, stone walls, and groups of Fresian cows which look as though they've been planted in a square field, all facing east. The Ullswater Steamer leaflet urges travellers to keep an eye out for Peregrine falcons, buzzards, ospreys and red squirrels. I don't see any, but that's a good excuse if I need one, to visit again.

It's like sailing through tranquillity itself, with the occasional spectacle of a waterfall, the 65ft high Aira Force is mid-way on the west, a red-sailed yacht, another ferry, with flag flying and walkers on the hills, scurrying along paths, through rocks that look as though they are bleeding silver blood as water spurts down the hills that are covered with yellow gorse and trees. And what trees! Yews that must have been here since the Viking days silver birch, firs, willow, oak, rowan, beech, hawthorn, ash and some I probably missed, all holding themselves up for inspection as we glided past.

Wordsworth was visiting Ullswater when he was stunned by the daffodils and he also wrote that 'it is the happiest combination of beauty and grandeur which any of the lakes affords' and he was an expert. Particularly in the 'wandered lonely as a cloud' bit; as we don't have one in the sky The ferry calls at Howtown, on its way where visitors can disembark and walk to Glenridding where it is possible to see Helvelly in the distance and note where Wordsworth and his sister, Dorothy, walked when they visited the area. Go in Spring and experience what he meant by those daffodils.

In contrast, Sir Donald Campbell set his speed record in Bluebird K7, a jet-propelled hydroplane, on this lake, which gives some idea of the extent of it. That must have frightened the skelly, a kind of fish that is found here. At Glenridding they think it must be a type of trout, but they aren't too sure. It is a white fish, according to my dictionary and so-called because of its large scales. They don't serve it in Pooley Bridge where they do have a wonderful memorial with a fish on top; it could a skelly, which reads: 'Pooley Mill Fish Cross/ Erected by /Berton Parish Council in the Millennium Year 2000 to commemorate the twelfth century charter granted by King John to hold a Fish Market in Pooley Village Square. The previous one was removed in 1860 to allow turning space for horses and coaches bringing visitors to Ullswater.'

They wouldn't have been able to cross the sixteenth century bridge over the river Eamont that leads from Pooley Bridge town to Ullswater. It's dangerous enough walking over, but luckily there are passing places.

There are plenty of pubs in Pooley Bridge where I decide to have a 'usquebaugh' as that is the Gaelic for whisky and although I'm not in Scotland, this drink tastes the same wherever it's drunk. There is no doubt that whisky is the biggest selling export in the world. I had a friend once who sold it in Italy. He said that a whisky was being sold in England at one stage with labels that stated it was made in Italy so they were all confiscated as no one is allowed to use the name Scotch, except the Scots. It is an acquired taste but it is a very satisfying drink (especially after a disappointing evening at a bridge club), if it is poured into a glass of warm milk. I doubt if Wordsworth in his poem, the 'Pet Lamb' where he hears a voice that says 'Drink, pretty creature, drink!' was either referring or talking to me, but I need no further encouragement. I didn't however, have a tot of the party drink I mixed once for some golfers I had staying. It was a recipe I found on 'SirCookalot' on line. I used my home made rosehip syrup with it and kept it well away from my father, who would not have been amused at good whisky being maltreated in this way and it's no way to treat rose hip syrup either. I mixed 2 bottles of whisky, (cheapest possible) with half a pound of caster sugar, four tablespoons honey, a small bottle cider and same of rosehip syrup , in a bowl and then bottled. This is sweet, extremely potent, and very popular with some. Smaller proportions may be used of course.

VAYNOR

'V' is Vaynor and chosen, not only because it is the only 'V' I can find in the right place, after Ullswater, but I had read 'How Green was my Valley' by Richard Llewellyn when I was about thirteen years old. It is said that the story was based on the author's experience of the valleys in South Wales so I'm here to relive the memories of Huw, the boy with whom I identified, who although male, always seemed to be at odds with something as I was. It was the destruction of his pencil box at the national school that I remembered best. 'Eighteen inches long and three wide, with a top that slid off and a piece cut out for your thumb to press it through the groove. On the top tray, three lovely red pencils, new and without the marks of teeth, with sharp points and two pens, green, with brass holders for nibs and the end a little pit for a piece of rubber. The top tray was fast on a pivot and you pushed it round to come to the second tray, with five more lovely pencils, three yellow and a red and a blue.' There were other things described too, compass, dividers, I think and ruler. I had one just like that, at boarding school, when I was six. I used the box as a dolls' house and put blotting paper under the pencils for their beds. But the shame when it was discovered, the mocking laughter of the rest of the class and the teacher telling me not to be such a baby, is still with me.

There was a film of the book with Walter Pigeon and Maureen O'Hara. This must have been the first film I ever saw and I would hate to see it again, because, from the vague memories I have, it was sentimental in the extreme. The Welsh valleys however, are very real and I wanted to experience them myself and try to find the slag heap that never actually covered Huw's village, but was always there, above and menacing. Huw's mother was very brave renouncing God when her husband died. There was another soulmate.   From Penrith to Cardiff, where not only is there a good selection of b and b's, but it is also an excellent place from which to explore South Wales by bus. One of these goes to Merthyr Tydfil, from opposite the station, but don't be fooled, once reaching this ex-iron and coal mining centre, into thinking that Vaynor, which is only a few miles up the road according to my map, is on anyone else's. There is no mention of it on the bus timetable and those in charge of the 'Blue box' of information, looked wildly around seeking inspiration when approached. Here it is; take the Pontsticill bus, which leaves fairly infrequently from the terminus. The driver will put you off on the corner of the crossroads into Vaynor, so that it is just a step to the Pontsarn Inn. Here the St Gwynno's trail, which sounded interesting, will take only one and a half hours, leaving plenty of time to catch the bus back to Merthyr Tydfil. Tell the driver of your intentions; I find all bus drivers incredibly helpful. St Gwynno is not the most famous of saints. There is a very beautiful little church in his name, at Llanwynno, just down the road, and here in Vaynor, he give his name to the pleasant walk of four miles long, exploring the green, green valley. He could have been Saxon, Welsh or even have come from Brittany, but it was believed he brought Christianity to this area in 874 AD. There is a feeling of well being about this hamlet which appears to have been created by the truth and reconciliation thinking that found its way here as early as the late nineteenth century and was based on good old socialism. Robert T Crawshay, a severe ironmaster of the day, who built the church at Vaynor, is buried here under a ten-ton stone slab inscribed with the words, 'God Forgive Me', which was a bit late, as he'd been very cruel to his workforce when alive. The fact that the grave is surrounded by iron railings shows that he was still afraid of his workers, from whom he barricaded himself while alive, but it is good to think that he regretted his cruel ways at the end.

    The Morgan family, in HGWMV, had a good life at the beginning of the book, plenty of food and many gold sovereigns, but although I could visualise them round the table in a shadowy miner's house on the hill, there was no slag heap and I had to admit this wasn't their village. Huw's father might have left his farm to work in the Merthyr Tydfil iron works though and he could have died in the mine that might have belonged to a man like Crawshay. Vaynor benefited from the success of Merthyr Tydfil by being able to provide the wealthy with agricultural produce and it has remained rural to this day. It had a wooden church built in 874 AD in honour of St Gwynno but this was burned down in 1291 and there is an intriguing grass mound in CarBurdydd, to be seen on the trail which is thought to hold the remains of a wooden castle predating the nearby Morlais Castle. A job for Tony Robinson?

There is an excellent view of Vaynor and the trail, which I photograph from the old disused quarry way up on the hill, where I remember part of a jolly poem by Harri Webb (1920 -96) an Anglo-Welsh poet who was active with Plaid Cymru It is the kind of poem that is easy to remember because of its rhythm, which, in this lyrical land is almost like a rugby song

'We started drinking at seven And went out for a breather at ten,
And all the stars in heaven said; Go back and drink again.
We were singers, strongmen and sages;./ We were witty and wise and brave/And all the ghosts of the ages / Applauded from Crawshay's grave.'
The poem ends with these words:
'and the stars of the Plough went swaggering, from Vaynor to Pengarnddu.' (taken from the 'Big Night',)
The 520 square miles of the Brecon Beacons National Park are full of reminders of the ancient past. There are prehistoric standing stones, medieval castles and many relics of the industrial age. But standing on any hill, it is the high mountains and moorland, peaceful valleys, farms full of sheep, woods and the inevitable water, with lakes and plunging waterfalls that impress. Vichy was the first mineral water I ever head of and this was a sparkling as any; far tastier too.

WESTON SUPER MARE.

There is a very good through Super Mare, the next letter to visit. They had advertised that their new Grand Pier would be open train from Newport to Weston from February 2008; the first one having been burnt down As piers are a traditional part of life in Britain and I enjoy them very much, this is a good place to go next.

They have an ancient and a modern pier in this town The ancient one at Clevedon has had a very chequered career. It collapsed in 1970 after a load testing for insurance purposes and took until 1998 before it opened again. It is now the only grade one listed pier that is open to the public in the country, the other one at Brighton having suffered the fate of so many piers and almost burnt down in 2002. In 1979 a National Pier Association was formed, with support from Sir John Betjeman, who wrote that 'Clevedon without a pier, would be like a diamond with a flaw.' Piers are subject to fires; there was a huge conflagration on the Great Yarmouth pier in 1954 when I happened to be staying at the time. Live flames flew across the street and appeared to be settling on the roof of our hotel. It was an anxious night. That pier has been rebuilt, like the Clevedon one, as these long arms into the sea hold a special place in people's lives.

There is something exciting about being in an amusement park over the sea, almost like indulging in a cruise but one that you can leave at any time. The Grand Pier in Weston Super Mare has survived two fires, one in 1930 which managed to re-open in 1933 when it lost its theatre and gained a fun fair instead and the one in 2008 which re-opened in 2010. There is a Gambling Bill that is due to be heard soon, and it is to be hoped that it will not result in the closure of slot machines in order to protect under 18s and presumably irresponsible grannies, but it might result also in a few more piers having to close if they lose this vital source of income.

The Grand Pier is not used for receiving ships, as was the original intent; that job is reserved for Clevedon, where the Waverley steamship visits annually, but the Grand Pier is full of people enjoying themselves enormously. I do something I've never done before; sit in a booth to have a portrait done in the style of Rembrandt, by an artist with a dismembered voice, for only £3. There is little relation to the famous artist that I can see. There are however, little donkeys on the beach below, giving rides, looking happy enough, sandcastles being built and kites, that can be bought from small shops along the front, flying in the breeze sent up from the Bristol Channel. My gran used to come to Weston Super Mare with her family for holidays at the Royal Hotel on South Parade and was here when the Grand Pier had an official opening in 1904. I stay at the hotel for this reason and one other. Gran had been visiting my parents in South Africa in 1940, when she had a terrible row with my father and decided to come back to Scotland. As she was going to take the mail boat, which they called the Union Castle line in those days, my parents tried to dissuade her, as there was a war on. I can still see her, sitting on the large verandah of the Durban Royal Hotel, her luggage round her feet, mouth set in a grim straight line, winning her argument, which she usually did. She was also making loud comments on the superiority of the Royal Hotel in Weston Super Mare with the one in Durban. Actually, she preferred everything in Britain which was the cause of the argument between her and my father in the first place.

Thanks to our global economy, there are mountains of watermelons at markets everywhere, as they are here, and there is no better thirst quencher than a watermelon 'slushie'. Liquidise 2 cups of seeded watermelon with 2 teaspoons of honey, and some crushed ice. Add a pinch of black pepper; serve with a mint sprig. I shall have to wait until I get home for this one; the hotel think I'm bonkers when I suggest it for breakfast. They have it at the Royal Hotel in Durban.

'XETER

That night I wrestle with my conscience about 'X'. I'd had a bet with a friend that I'd find an X somewhere in England, but I couldn't. I've had an idea though. It is but an hour and three quarters to Exeter by rail from Weston Super Mare. I'll just drop the E and put in an apostrophe. 'Xeter'; nothing wrong with that. With the average greengrocer able to throw apostrophes about, it's now my turn. It is the right place to put an inscrutable letter of the alphabet too. X indicates a mystery of sorts and here there are plenty. Exeter is a city like many others, of tremendous variety, with over 600 shops, open air markets, antique and curio shops, collectors' fairs and large department stores ; there's nothing much new there then. But wait.

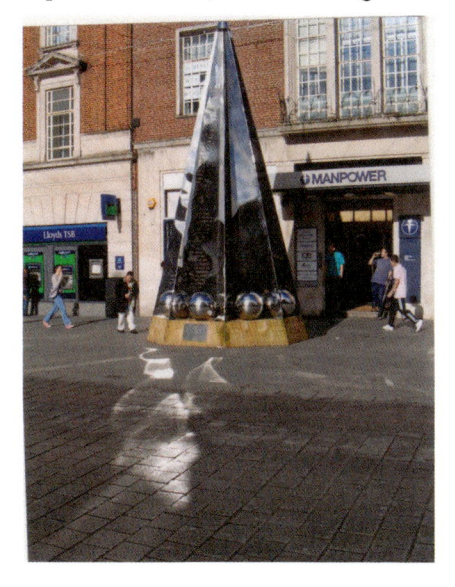

Walk down the High Street and you cannot miss a unique and stunning six and a half metre-high stainless steel sculpture designed by the sculptor Michael Fairfax, the Exeter riddle sculpture, stainless steel and stone. There are eight panels, each with a laser cut into the stainless steel in mirror writing. The panel opposite reflects the words so they can be read. The spheres at the base hold the answers to the riddles; these are reflected onto the panels. The riddles are from the 9th century Exeter Book which contains approximately 90 riddles. Here's one to solve; it's No.11

My garb is ashen and in my garments/bright jewels, garnet-coloured, gleam./I mislead muddlers, despatch the thoughtless/on fool's errands, and thwart cautious men/in their useful journeys. I can't think/why, addled and led astray, robbed/of their senses, men praise my ways/to everyone. Woe betide addicts/when they bring the dearest of hoards on high unless they've foregone their foolish habits. (answer wine.)

This sculpture is the centrepiece of the High Street improvement works and certainly catches my eye, but not many people I speak to, knows what the writing is all about. The answers to it all can be found at the West Country Studies library just off the High Street. There is one that has to be read to be believed. It is all about Lot in the cave with his daughters- in-law and is very rude.

Exeter is well placed for a leap into the West Country if you have time to explore and friends can lend you a typical Devon cottage in a typical Devon village, like that of East Ogwell for instance, just outside Newton Abbott, half an hour from Exeter. From here I was able to explore at leisure. It is possible to experience not only nearby Dartmoor, but the unique hospitality of people who seem to know what life's all about. Small country buses are alive and well, as evidenced by Eddie's local one, which not only collects anyone from the village who stands looking hopefully, but will remind regulars that they need to get off here, as it is their library day, had they forgotten?

The Dart river is an explorer's heaven. Alice Oswald wrote a long poem as she walked along the banks from the source to Dartmouth on the coast, telling of all the people and places that she met on the way The great joy of Dartmoor is that a car is not necessary. Traveline gives details of all the places that can be visited by train or bus, including Widdecome in-the-Moor, which is in an almost inaccessible valley. Buckfastleigh Abbey is a disappointment, as I go to see the famous bees that have been there for so long, looked after by the monk, Brother Adam for seventy years, but they had closed them to visitors because of the Health and Safety Act. The Xhosas in Africa, make the most wonderful wine from honey, as the Saxons obviously did and the monks on Holy Island, and is sometimes called mead. The Xhosa wine is called iQhilika and you need to be able to 'click' before you can pronounce this. It is made from wild or semi-wild hives and is rich in pollen and debris. They export a little to the States, but not on the scale that other South African wines are sold; it is usually consumed immediately, and with good reason.

YEOVILLE

South Western trains run regularly from Exeter to 'Y' Yeovil.. Somerset and cider are almost synonymous, who can ever forget the Wurzels singing? 'I am a cider drinker/ I drinks it all of the day/ I am a cider drinker/ It soothes all me troubles away/: Oh arr oh arr aay/;/: Oh arr oh arr aay;

Or in more serious vein, John Philips' poem 'Cider',

'...be thou the copious matter of my song,/And thy choice nectar; on which always waits/ Laughter, and sport, and care-beguiling wit,/and friendship, chief delight of human life/Why should we wish for more?'

Why indeed risk drinking anything other than pure cider that comes from our own earth, it's 'choice nectar', which is better than any foreign wine? Somerset cider is said to be dry and sparkling and a more cultured version than the average. There are many types; traditional cider is light dry, effervescent and appeals to true cider connoisseurs. My son-in-law, who is a cider drinker, says that Dabinett Apple Cider is a good one, with a great oaky aftertaste, a little sweeter than the French equivalent, which, unpatriotically, he prefers. It is good to pay a visit to Perry's Cider Mills at Ilminster in the autumn when cider making takes place. There is a great selection of draught and bottled ciders which may be sampled before buying. It's when we come to drinking scrumpy that we need to be as strong as the drink itself, and sharp. It is made of crab apples without sugar. Its name comes from the fact that farm workers 'scrumped' or stole apples from the orchard to make it. Cyser is a sweet cider, a bit like sherry and very good with desserts. It is a blend of pure vintage apple juice and wildflower honey, fermented slowly in a way that dates back to Viking times. There was some good in them then.

For the 'spritzer' kind of drinker, berry cider is the nearest equivalent as it is a blend of apple cider and the unfermented juices of berries and fruits.   The Romans made their mark in this area and it was thought they brought their own apple trees with them. But that's not all they brought. When I make apple juice, as I did in Alton, I worry about what to do with the apple pulp that is left over. Now the Romans gave Britain many things and one of them is 'The Gift of the Gods' which was a valuable medicine for them. This wasn't cider, it was yoghurt, which is one of the oldest foods know to man and has been a basic nutritional product in Europe, the Middle East and Central Asia for thousands of years. In 76 BC, the Roman historian Plinius recommended 'the administration of fermented milk products for treating gastroenteritis'. So all those TV advertisements about a yoghurt drink, mixed with all sorts of fruit, may have something in them after all.   I love yoghurt, with stewed fruit; yoghurt can be made at home as well, although there are special yoghurt makers now for sale. But I use a slow cooker, putting 4 cups whole milk on low for 2 and half hours. Unplug and cool for three hours. Add half a cup of shop-bought live yoghurt, mix with two cups of the milk, then return to the slow cooker, keep unplugged, wrap in a thick towel and let it sit for eight hours; overnight is good. You should have yoghurt the next morning and the fact that it's taken nearly a whole day to prepare, seems to add to the flavour. It is perfect for a 'smoothie' drink, with any fruit, particularly apple.

ZEAL

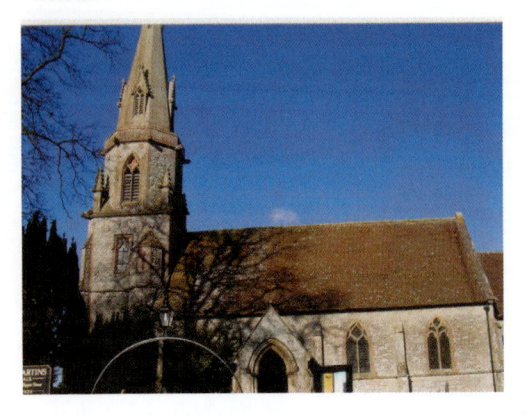

Nobody thought I'd find a 'Z' at all, let alone one in the right place to lead me back home. But there it is, Zeal in Wilshire. Using Somerset First Bus Service, 58A, it takes about an hour and a half to reach the end of the alphabet and my wonderful journey. It was even more exciting to discover that the church in Zeal is a fine example of architecture by George Gilbert Scott and dedicated to St Martin. Some saints are suspect in their origins and as a seeker after truth and descended from clergymen of all sorts, I am inclined to view them either with scepticism or admiration, as in the case of St Etheldreda of Ely and now of St Martin. He is a saint with whom many people, including me, can identify. He was a great guy and knew how to deal with the Devil. The saint was an avid walker and once on his way to Rome, legend has it that he met Satan on the way. The Devil taunted the holy man for not using some kind of conveyance which would be more suited to a bishop. St Martin immediately changed the Old Serpent into a mule and, jumping on its back, trotted along happily. Whenever the devil slackened pace, Martin urged it on to full speed, making the sign of the cross, thus defeating Satan at all turns. The Devil, who showed a rather clever literary bent, then exclaimed:

Signa te Signa, temere me tangis et angis/Roma tigi subito motibus igit amor

How's that for two palindromes? The translation is very boring subito motibus.. 'Cross, cross thyself: thou plaguest and vexest me without necessity for owing to my exertions, thou wilt soon reach Rome, the object of thy wishes.' St Martin was a genial man which may be why he is popular in England. There are seven churches in London and Westminster dedicated to him.

When St Giles took over the protection of beggars, St Martin became the patron saint of publicans, tavern-keepers and other dispensers of good eating and drinking. In the hall of the Vintners' Company of London, paintings and statues of St Martin and Bacchus hang amicably side by side.

Zeal church is sensible claiming this saint, whose day is marked by November 11th; a day we all remember for another reason. But it is also the day that new wines of the year are drawn from the lees and tasted. English wine is now come of age and many awards have been won by growers from the Wessex region There are thirty members of this Association and to quote one member, Paul Langham of Beckett's Vineyard in Wiltshire, 'In this region we can really hold our heads up now'. As long as we don't overdo the wine, of course. St Martin would be pleased, especially when the Temperance Band that had been formed before the First World War gave up the ghost and was renamed the Zeal St Martin's Silver Band in 1930. Church services are not as well attended as they used to be, and the buildings are very often full of people who merely want to admire the architecture, stained glass windows, pictures and statues of saints, or to catch breath before going home. Nothing wrong with any of that, particularly in a church dedicated to a saint who does not frown on having the odd tipple. Beer is still the most popular drink in Britain, and according to Wikipedia, in the world. It dates back to the time when cereal was first farmed. One of the most interesting beers is made by the Zulus, in Kwa/Zulu Natal, South Africa. We used to farm there and the workers made their own beer on the farm, from sorghum, which is a tropical cereal. It is usually brewed by women in a special hut that is not completely thatched so that smoke can escape and the beer ferments with sufficient oxygen available. I'm not sure our health and safety rules would allow us to make beer in the same way, but it works a treat in Africa. This brew is called Utshwala. Maize and sorghum are cooked to form a thick porridge, then left to stand for one day to steep, on the second day the softened grains are boiled with water to form a milky soup and dried sorghum is sprinkled on top. The large pot is covered to keep it warm and aid the fermentation process (also to keep flies and dust off). The liquid is then filtered through a grass sieve. Mageu is another type of beer they used to make, using similar quantities of mealie meal, (a fine maize) and ground malt with a third of water. They fermented this and if it was too thick to pour, they added more water. My children , who don't appear to have suffered from it, now tell me that they often had a mugful, unknown to me at the time.

ALTON isn't very far away and I'm home by evening. One of the more interesting things to do on a long journey, especially if it is a bit bumpy and reading is difficult, is to compose a haiku for places visited. They are composed of seventeen syllables in three lines, five in the first and last and seven in the middle. According to the Japanese, where they originated, it is necessary to mention the season somewhere; something like this:

'Purple yellow, white/Garish in the pale green grass/Defying summer.'

They don't need to be good, just a reminder of a happy moment. This was an effort written when the purple loosestrife was so beautiful on the way from Laurence Kirk to Nairn.

Hampshire is one of Britain's most pleasing counties and gives rise to my last haiku on this trip. Wildlife and footpaths/ Welcoming trees and sunshine/ Such joy to be home.

Printed in Great Britain
by Amazon